LOOKING

BACK

MEMORIES
OF
PALMYRA, ILLINOIS

LARRY P. MAHAN

Larry P. Mahan

TRUTH BOOK PUBLISHERS

ISBN: 978-1-940725-29-1

Truth Book Publishers
Franklin, IL 62638
www.truthbookpublishers.com
877-649-9092

Printed in the United States of America.

Dedication

To my loving wife, Donna, who inspired me to write this book and spent countless hours editing the manuscript.

To my three children: Brad, Rene, and Angie-Thanks for your love and support along the way.

To my grandchildren: Colt, Ryan, Grant, and Madeleine-May you always cherish your family history.

Acknowledgments

Writing a book like this would not have been possible without the support of family and friends.

Verifying historical information, gathering pictures and corroborating my memory of childhood events required many hours of research and many pleasant visits and phone conversations with those who were involved or had knowledge of the events recounted here.

The people who have contributed to this book are too numerous to mention, and I know I would surely leave some people out if I tried to provide such a list. Thank you very much to everyone who provided assistance in big ways and small. I am greatly appreciative and I hope you enjoy this book!

Larry P. Mahan

Norma Solomon Scroggins

In Appreciation...

I spent numerous hours gathering information about North and South Palmyra Townships, the early history of Palmyra, and the Palmyra that I knew as a child. I was very fortunate to have access to Norma (Solomon) Scroggins' memories and her extensive collection of historical articles and pictures. Norma, a warm and jovial person, always greeted my visits with a cheerful, "What have you got today!"

Norma (Solomon) Scroggins was born in 1927 to Elbert and Opal Solomon in the Palmyra home where she now resides. Norma's ancestry goes back to Judge Lewis Solomon, her great-great-grandfather, one of the early settlers in North Palmyra Township. D.N. Solomon, Norma's great-granduncle, along with two other men, was responsible for surveying and plotting the current town of Palmyra, Illinois.

Norma married Dayle "Cinny" Scroggins in 1950, and they were blessed with five children; Ed, Bob, Ann, Mary and Gayle. "Cinny" passed away in 1982. Norma's career experiences included working for the Red Cross in St. Louis, Missouri; as a meat wrapper and bookkeeper at the Macoupin Locker in Palmyra, Illinois; and twenty three years as head cook at the Silver Strands Senior Citizens Center in Palmyra until she retired in 2002.

Norma was an invaluable resource as we spent many happy hours talking about old times.

Thanks, Norma...

Reference Materials

The following resources were used in my research for this book.

1. Old Weekly Transcript newspapers from Palmyra, Illinois. The Transcript office closed in 1970 after eighty years of printing local news.
2. 1875 Macoupin County Atlas—Contains old land settlements, hand sketched family farms, plots of townships, towns, and villages, and itemized lists of businesses during that era.
3. Macoupin County Historical Society archival records.
4. Numerous articles, pictures and stories that Norma (Solomon) Scroggins collected during her lifetime.
5. Conversations with classmates and friends to help verify many of my childhood memories.

LOOKING

BACK

MEMORIES
OF
PALMYRA, ILLINOIS

Contents

My Parents

Early Life

Move to the Farm

Back to Palmyra

History of North and South Palmyra Townships

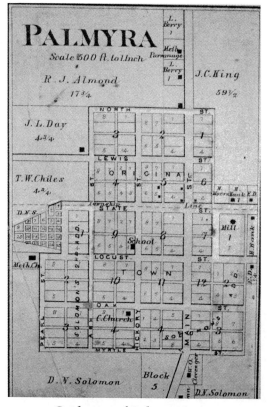

Grid map of Palmyra, 1870

History of North and South Palmyra Townships

Illinois became the 21st state in 1818. Later, after county and township boundary lines were established, settlers began arriving in great numbers. It was the arduous task of surveyors to establish boundaries for prospective landowners.

North Palmyra Township
(Township 12-Range 8 West)

General Facts

1. John Cummings and Jonas Thompson were the first settlers (squatters) to arrive in 1824, followed by Woodring in 1825, Wills in 1826, and Solomon, Thompson, Springer, Nevins, and others in 1827.
2. Because creeks provided the necessary water supply, settlers often built their cabins near the following watersheds: Solomon, Joes, Apple, and Massey (now called Nassa) Creeks.
3. A limited number of Pottawattamie Indians lived in North Palmyra Township.

Firsts in North Palmyra Township

1. Jonathan Thompson was the first to purchase land (section 4) in 1827.
2. Lewis Solomon's farm (section 20), known as Eagle's Point, housed the first post office at his home. He was the first Justice of the Peace and a local creek was named for him.
3. The first school, established in 1829, was located at the northwest area of Section 18.
4. E.C. Vancil had the first horse driven corn grinding mill.
5. The first church, Bethel Methodist, was built in 1840 and was later used as a rural school.

The population of North Palmyra Township in 1870 was approximately 1,200 people.

South Palmyra Township
(Township 11-Range 8 West)

General Facts

1. Seth Hodges and John Love were the first settlers (squatters) to arrive in 1815 and 1816, followed by Taylor in 1823, Day in 1824, Matthews in 1827, Hoover in 1829, Massey in 1829, Ross in 1829, Cave in 1830, and others.
2. The all- important watersheds included the following: Hodges (now called Otter), Massey (now called Nassa), and Solomon Creeks.
3. A few Pottawattamie Indians lived in various locations throughout South Palmyra Township.

Firsts in South Palmyra Township

1. David Taylor was the first Justice of the Peace in 1823.
2. Felix Hoover was the first to use a sod plow to plant wheat in 1830.
3. Massey Creek was named for Isaac Massey, but was later changed to Nassa Creek.
4. The first School, established in1831, was a log cabin in southern South Palmyra Township.
5. The first church, Concord Primitive, was established in 1829, four miles south of Palmyra.
6. Andrew Russell owned the first grinding mill.

The population of South Palmyra Township in 1870 was approximately 1,150 people.

History of Palmyra

Dopheide Wagon Factory, 1861

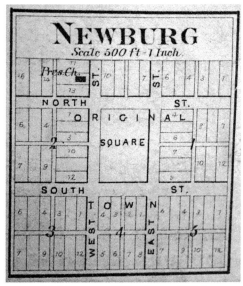

Grid map of Newberg, 1835

History of Palmyra

The origin of the village of Palmyra began in 1835 when James Cave, with help from Benjamin Stephenson, surveyed plots located on Section 4 in South Palmyra Township. The area was comprised of fifty six lots and a town square and was located just east of today's old city park. Newburg was the name of the early settlement as it was recorded in 1836.

Just So You Know

1. William Owen built the first log home.
2. A stage coach route, operating from Jacksonville to Carlinville, stopped at Owen's home twice a week to exchange horse teams.
3. Oakes Shaw, the Palmyra Postmaster in 1841, used his home as the first post office. James Gardner used a

public building when he became the next Postmaster.
4. Newspapers, delivered by stage coach, were a rarity.
5. Early businesses included a hotel, merchandise store, blacksmith shop, and an elementary school in a log cabin.
6. Dr. Thornton, the first doctor, came in 1840.

In 1842, residents of Newburg were informed by the State of Illinois that another town in Illinois already had the name of Newburg. After much consideration, Cummington was voted the new village name.

Thirteen years later, after several wet springs emphasized the drawbacks of being located in a low terrain, three leading citizens, D.N. Solomon, J.F. Nifong, and Hezekiah Berry, were given the task of finding a better location for the village. Within a few months a new site was selected. In 1854, plans were made to move Cummington to higher ground, just over half a mile to the west.

Solomon quickly developed a public square, located at the southeast corner of Main and State Streets, and after the plot was recorded in early 1855 the new settlement became known as Palmyra. Tradition ascribes the selected name as a tribute to the Solomon family, founder of Palmyra, Syria. As D.N. Solomon continued to establish lots for the southern part of Palmyra, J.F. Nifong and Hezekiah Berry did the same for the northern region of town.

Solomon Homestead-Oldest house in Palmyra, 1856

By the end of 1855, Solomon had constructed a two-story building at the southwest corner of Main and State Streets. Within a few weeks, the new store was completely stocked and open for business. Later, Solomon built his new home (which still stands today), just half a block south of his business. In 1856, Nifong built his residence just west of the northwest corner of Main and State Streets.

Early Businesses

1. 1855-R.F. Braken built a hotel on the north side of East State Street.
2. 1856-Fordyce Shaw, D.N. Solomon, and A.C. Farmer built a grist mill, followed by a carding mill, and a saw mill.

Malone & Son Blacksmith Shop, 1859

3. 1859-Malone's blacksmith shop was established.
4. 1861-Ernest Dopheide became known in central Illinois for his "Dopheide Wagons".

T.W. Chiles Mercantile building, 1862.
Present day Palmyra Opera House.

5. 1862-T.W. Chiles moved his mercantile business from Cummington to the northeast corner of Main and State Streets in Palmyra. (Today's Opera House Restaurant).
6. 1863-Sterling Berry opened the first furniture store and coffin business.

The Martin Block, 1868.

7. 1868-Fire destroyed the D.N. Solomon building. W.C. Martin joined Solomon and new buildings were erected on the same site. Later, Martin became the sole owner.

Early Doctors

1. 1861-G. Allmond, followed by Van Winkle & Morrison.
2. 1870-'90-Day, Wilson, Carlisle, Sprinkle, Thomas, Allen, and Faith.
3. Later-McMahan, Powell, Hudson, Crum, and Neese.

Dentists

1. 1880-Gilder, followed by Allen.

Early Churches

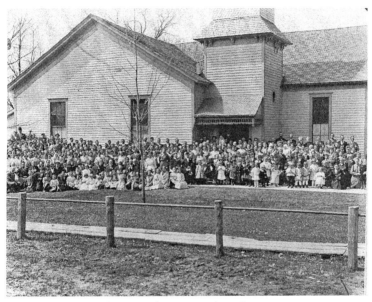

Palmyra Christian Church, 1867

1. 1867-The Christian Church was the first church in Palmyra and was located at the southwest part of town. It burned in 1922 and was rebuilt in 1923 at the present location.

Palmyra Methodist Church, 1869

2. 1869-The Methodist Church was built at the west part
   of town, at the corner of Pearl and Locust Streets. In
   1910, Etta Hanshaw donated $14,000 to build a new
   brick church at the present location at the corner of
   Main and Lewis Streets.
3. 1878-The Cumberland Presbyterian Church was built
   and later became an Apostolic church.

Palmyra Baptist Church, 1908

4. 1884-The Baptist Church was built, and was enlarged in 1908.

Early Schools

1. 1856-'77- There were a few scattered one room log structures.
2. 1878- A new two-room school was located on the west side of town.
3. 1888-Two additional rooms were added to the existing school building.

Palmyra Public School, 1910

4. 1910-Palmyra Public School was built on the west side of town at the corner of Hickory and Locust Streets.
5. 1920-A community high school was built just southwest of the present Northwestern High School.

Palmyra High School, 1935

6. 1935- Palmyra High School was built in the southwest part of town.
7. 1948-Northwestern C.U. #2 was created with the consolidation of four area towns (Hettick, Palmyra, Modesto, and Scottville).

Cemeteries

Old Union Cemetery, 1836

1. Old Union Cemetery, the oldest Palmyra cemetery, was
    established in 1836 and the earliest burials were in the
    late 1830s. The cemetery was deeded to the town of
    Palmyra in 1862.

Oak Hill Cemetery, 1888

2. Oak Hill Cemetery was developed by D.N. Solomon in 1888. The Solomon addition was later joined by J.C. King (King Addition) to form the beginning of today's city cemetery.

<u>Later Businesses</u>

1. 1880-James Duncan, Eli Richie, and Thomas Mahan started the first lumber company.

Allen Brothers Dry Goods Store, 1882

2. 1882-Allen Brothers Dry Goods was located on the southeast corner of Main and State Streets. (Later, this became Dad's clothing store that burned in 1951).
3. 1883-D.N. Solomon built a two-story building just south of his old building. This was the first Opera House and it hosted the first high school commencement.
4. 1883-Richie & King Grocery Store was a brick building on the north side of East State Street.
5. 1902-Grimmett & Waters General Store was on the northeast corner of Main and State Streets.

R.R. Ragan Hardware Store, 1880s

In 1926, a disastrous fire destroyed six businesses located on the north side of East State Street, half a block east of the Grimmett & Waters building. Those businesses that lay in ruins included: W.E. Berryman's Barber Shop, Kuehl's Bakery, Standefer's Restaurant, Alonza Moore's Pool Room, Joseph Manger's Harness Shop, and C.H. Shumway's Implement Store.

Old Downtown Palmyra, early 1900s

C.P. & St.L. Railroad

Palmyra Depot, 1890s

The Chicago to Peoria to St. Louis railroad was completed in 1881. Towns along the rail line quickly flourished as local farm products served the needs of larger metropolitan areas. The C.P. & St.L. was temporarily closed in 1926, until the selling of bonds enabled the railroad to reopen. Businesses continued to prosper until the coming of the Great Depression of the 1930s. With the arrival of freight trucks and the slow recovery from the depression, the railroad suffered greatly. In 1941, the C.P. & St.L. closed for good as Motor Car #15 made its final run through Palmyra.

Roy Neece-railroad worker, early 1900s

Communications

1. 1890-The first newspaper was published by George Goodhead; later it became Spooner's Weekly Transcript
2. Mid-1890s-The Telegraph Office was operated by V.N. Hinkle.
3. 1897-The Telephone Office was located above A. Allen's Store at the southeast corner of Main and State Streets.

Banks

1. 1881- The Bank of Palmyra was located near today's Palmyra Christian Church. Later a new building was constructed on North Main Street, half of a block north of the intersection of Main and State Streets.
2. 1912-The People's Bank was located on the north side of East State Street. (Later it became a tavern).
3. 1925-The Bank of Palmyra and The People's Bank merged, forming the Bank of Palmyra.
4. 1931-The Bank of Palmyra closed due to the depression. The building became Lampley's Drug Store in the late 1930's. In the mid 1940's, George Hargett became the new owner of Hargett's Drug Store.
5. Palmyra was without a bank until May, 1952.

Aerial Photo of Palmyra, 1929

The population of Palmyra in 1890 was listed as 1,527.

Firsts

1. 1855-The first child, Ellen Berry, was born in Palmyra to Mr. & Mrs. Hezekiah Berry.
2. 1859-W.W. Rhodes operated a coal powered electric plant.

Thomas and Sarah Mahan

3. 1860s-Thomas and Sarah Mahan settled just north of the Blooming Grove area.

Allen Brothers Store, 1882

4. 1881-The first brick building was Allen Brother's Store. (Later, Mahan's Clothing Store).
5. 1900-CIPS provided a limited quantity of electric power.

East State Street, 1916

6. 1901-Downtown Palmyra received concrete sidewalks.

Nifong Wrecker Service, 1920s

7. 1920-K.L. & Roy Nifong built a modern auto garage on north Main Street. Today, Jennings' Chevrolet occupies that site.

State Route 111 construction through Palmyra, 1931

8. 1931-State Route 111 was completed through Palmyra.

Stults Funeral Home, 1932

9. 1932-Stults Brothers opened a funeral home on north Main Street.
10. 1940-A modern fire engine, gasoline powered, replaced an old 1927 hand pump model.

Terry Park

Old Terry Park House, 1837

In 1837, Lewis O'Neal settled forty acres of timber land one and a half miles east of Palmyra. Before his death in 1854, the O'Neal's had acquired an additional three hundred sixty acres. After Mrs. O'Neal's death in 1892, Mrs. Jenny (O'Neal) Terry inherited the farm place and eighty acres. When Mrs. Terry died in 1926, her farm was willed to the Village of Palmyra, to be used as a public park and cemetery.

Old Terry Park Cabin, 1940

During the depression in the early 1930s, Palmyra received government grants, plus the use of the W.P.A., to remove timber and build a new lake. Later, a nine- hole golf course (sand greens) was added, along with tennis courts and a ball field. In the 1940s, Miss Florence O'Neal, last surviving member of the Lewis O'Neal family, donated logs that were used to build the Terry Park log cabin.

In 1948, the Village of Palmyra held its first picnic at Terry Park to raise money for the park upkeep. Then in 1949, Terry Park was designated as the ideal place for the Macoupin County Junior Fair. Because of the success of the "Junior Fair", Palmyra decided to continue the event annually but change the name to the Terry Park Fair. Under the direction of Mayor Oral Cooper, the Terry Park Community Club and other civic organizations were able to create an outstanding small town fair that attracted many visitors from surrounding towns. The annual Terry Park Fair closed in 1992, shortly after the death of Mayor Cooper.

Today, Terry Park is known for its architecturally landscaped golf course and a modern clubhouse.

My Parents

Paul & Lucille Mahan, married in 1933

Paul Marvin Mahan

Walter Scott & Ella (Holiday) Mahan

Dad was born at home on June 7, 1912 to Walter Scott and Ella (Holliday) Mahan. The attending physician, Dr. William L. Powell, drove more than four miles by horse and buggy to the Blooming Grove area to deliver his future son-in-law.

L-R: Stanley, Walter, & Paul Mahan

Dad's family consisted of his parents and a brother, Stanley, who was thirteen months older than him. The Mahan farm was located just north of the Blooming Grove School, where Uncle Stanley and Dad received their elementary education. Just across the road from the school was the Blooming Grove Christian Church, where Dad and his family attended.

Mahan Homestead, Blooming Grove area, 1860

Blooming Grove School

Blooming Grove Church

Besides farming, Grandpa Mahan supervised the use of a beacon light for the U.S. Mail Service. A tower was erected on his farm in late 1925 and Grandpa was paid a monthly stipend to maintain the kerosene lamp that was hoisted up and into the huge red globe each evening.

Beacon lights were strategically placed between St. Louis and Chicago, as they helped guide night flights that were delivering U.S. mail. One of the young pilots at that time was little known, Charles A. Lindbergh. On one occasion, Lindbergh landed his plane on Grandpa's farm for a maintenance check. Grandpa, Uncle Stanley (15), and Dad (14), escorted Lindbergh by wagon to Palmyra for supplies. Upon hearing that a plane had landed on Grandpa's farm, several people rode horseback to the Mahan farm to watch Lindbergh take off.

Paul in his baseball uniform

Dad was active in sports even at an early age. When he started high school in Palmyra in 1927 he played football and track, but baseball was his love. Dad's other love was

Lucille Powell, who he began dating during his sophomore year (Mother was a senior) in high school. Dad became the star pitcher for the Palmyra High School Panthers.

Paul in his college days

After graduation from high school, Dad enrolled at Lincoln College, Lincoln, Illinois, where he pursued a two-year business degree. During his college years at Lincoln, Dad continued to date Mother, who was attending Eureka College. It was less than an hour's drive to Eureka, and Dad became a frequent visitor when his baseball schedule didn't interfere. When he stayed overnight in Eureka he often stayed at a men's fraternity house where Ronald "Dutch" Reagan lived.

Paul's first store

Dad became Lincoln's premier baseball pitcher and at the conclusion of his college career, he received a letter from the St. Louis Cardinals inviting him to a minor league baseball tryout. Dad was elated at the possibility of playing for the Cardinals, but Grandpa Mahan had different ideas. Grandpa thought Dad needed a "respectable" job, so he offered to help Dad open a men's clothing store in Palmyra. Because of Grandpa's insistence and the fact that Mom had accepted a teaching position near Palmyra, Dad decided to move back home. Within a few months Dad opened Mahan's Clothing Store in a small vacant building on the north side of East State Street. Then, on August 15, 1933, Dad and Mom were married at the Palmyra Christian Church. For the next two years they lived with Grandpa and Grandma Powell before moving to their first home, located at the southeast corner of Union and Myrtle streets in Palmyra.

Paul & Lucille as a young married couple, 1933

Dad's clothing store attracted customers from several surrounding communities because he carried work clothes with names like Carhartt, Red Wing, Red Ball, and Rockford & Rand. As he increased his stock, Dad's little store became too small, and when the Allen Brothers store became available in the early 1940's, Dad moved across the street to the two- story brick building (southeast corner of Main and State streets). Dad's new store provided twice as much storage space and enabled him to carry a larger selection of merchandise.

1ˢᵗ Terry Park Night Golf Tournament, 1950s.
Paul is kneeling on the far left.

Dad remained devoted to sports of all kinds. He continued playing baseball for an area men's team until he was almost forty years of age, and also won several horseshoe pitching contests. He was an avid St. Louis Cardinals baseball fan, and also enjoyed hunting, fishing, and golfing.

Paul with his hunting dog and trophies

Mahan Family Picture.
Lucille, Paul, Roger, Larry, & Scott, 1950

Dad was a strict disciplinarian who taught his three boys to respect the old, the young, the disadvantaged, and people of minority cultures. Dad spent a lifetime secretly helping those in need.

After the 1951 fire, Dad bought the O.J. Miller Hardware Store, just east of his old location that lay in ruins. Dad continued to operate Mahan's Clothing Store until his death on June 10, 1967.

Mary Lucille (Abner-Powell) Mahan

Lucille (L), with her mother and two brothers, 1912

Mom was born in Rockbridge, Illinois on September 1, 1910 to Gus and Lulu (Hardin) Abner. Later, the Abner family, including an older brother, Carl, and a younger brother, Edwin, moved to Summerville, Illinois.

In 1915, Lulu died from tuberculosis, leaving three young children with a father who was unable and/or unwilling to care for them. Each child was put in separate orphanages and Gus took off for parts unknown.

Enter the Powells

William Lightfoot Powell was born in 1860 near Longwood, Missouri. He received his elementary education in schools near his home, and attended pre-medical school in Indianapolis, Indiana.

William Lightfoot Powell as a young man, 1880

At that time he met Mary V. Spencer of Lawrenceville, Illinois and they were married in 1884. One year later, a son, Harry Lawrence, was born, only to die in 1890 from a childhood disease. William L. Powell began medical studies at the Bennett Medical College (Chicago) in the early 1890's. While he continued his medical studies in Chicago, Dr. Powell began his medical internship at Mt. Vernon, Missouri from 1893-'96. Dr. Powell's first birth delivery took place in 1893.

Dr. Powell with his medical bag, 1940s

Doctor and Mrs. Powell moved to Scottville, Illinois in 1897 where Dr. Powell began his medical practice while finishing his medical degree in Chicago. After serving the Scottville community for nine years, the Powell's moved to Palmyra, Illinois in 1906 where Dr. Powell continued his medical practice for another forty years. During his medical career, Dr. Powell delivered a total of one thousand two hundred and ninety six babies. His last delivery occurred just four months before he died at the ripe old age of eighty six. Dr. Powell served as elder of the Palmyra Christian Church and was also a former mayor of Palmyra.

Enter Mary Lucille Abner

Lucille as a young child

It had been twenty six long years since the Powell's had lost their only child, Harry Lawrence. Since the death of her son, Mrs. Powell had been unable to conceive again, causing her to suffer periods of depression. Then, in 1916, when they were both fifty six years old, the Powell's received word that a young girl had recently arrived at an orphan's home in St. Louis, Missouri. Still eager for a family, the Powell's adopted mother on September 1, 1916, the date given as her birthdate, although there was some question about this because of incomplete orphanage records. Soon after she moved to Palmyra, an uncle from Alton visited the Powell residence, hoping to maintain contact and visit with his niece. Instead, Grandpa Powell offered the visitor a hefty amount of money to leave and never return. Mom's uncle agreed.

Lucille in elementary school

Mother attended Palmyra Grade School (1916-1924) and graduated from Palmyra High School in 1928.

Lucille as a young lady

While attending high school, Mom excelled in music, especially as a piano player. Mom dated Dad during her senior year.

Lucille in her college days

In the fall of 1928, Mother enrolled at Eureka College, Eureka, Illinois, where she majored in music and general education. While attending Eureka College Mother became friends with Ronald "Dutch" Reagan, who went on to become the 40th President of the United States. When Dad visited Mother at Eureka, he frequently stayed at the fraternity house where Reagan lived.

Hazel Green, a one-room school house where Lucille taught

After graduating from Eureka in 1932, Mom moved back home with the Powell's to start her teaching career. During those early years, Mother taught elementary grades at Duncan and Hazel Green schools, located southeast of Palmyra. Mother often rode side saddle to work, using the school's stable (shelter and feed) for her horse.

Lucille in her wedding dress, 1933

Mom and Dad married on August 15, 1933 and they lived with Grandpa and Grandma Powell for about two years. Later, Mother continued her teaching career at the Palmyra Grade School while Dad operated Mahan's Shoe and Clothing Store in Palmyra. After the Northwestern Unit #2 consolidation in 1948, Mother taught grade school music in all four towns (Hettick, Palmyra, Modesto, and Scottville) as well as high school music at Northwestern High School.

Paul & Lucille Mahan, 1963 (30ᵗʰ Anniversary)

Mother taught a total of thirty three years (between the births of three children) and mentored several high school singing groups that received superior ratings at the Illinois High School State Association Music Contests. Outside of school, Mom enjoyed her church work, Eastern Star, and chauffeuring her lady friends to the Muni Opera and on shopping excursions.

Powell/Mahan Family Photo, 1939

Mother spent many fruitless years searching for her father and two brothers, but was never able to contact them. This early trauma in her life helped to foster frequent occurrences of loneliness, insecurity, and anxiety in her adult life.

Postscript:

In 1981 Mother was a judge of the amateur talent contest at the Terry Park Fair. As Mother was handing out awards, she noticed a name tag on a little girl with the last name of Abner. Mother mentioned to the little girl that her name was also Abner when she was a young girl growing up near Medora, Illinois. Later, as the little girl's family was driving home, she gave the information about the judge, Lucille Mahan, to her parents. Terry Abner, the father, immediately remembered past stories about the Gus/Lulu family. Mother received a telephone call the next day inquiring about her early childhood history. When Mother told Terry Abner that as a young child she lived in Summerville, Terry blurted out, "You must be "lost" Lucille."

Abner Family Reunion, 1980

Within two months an Abner family reunion was held at a park near Alton, Illinois. Several members of Mother's biological family attended, including her Uncle Fred, Gus Abner's brother, who had tried to visit her when she was a little girl. Also at the reunion were several cousins from the Alton/St. Louis area, a step-brother Bill (Beulah) Abner from Benson, Minnesota, and a step-sister, Helen (Abner) Reyer from Yakima, Washington.

Bill & Beulah Abner with Lucille, 1980

Mother had a wonderful day as her relatives discussed what they remembered about the Gus/Lulu Abner family. Evidently, after Gus put the three children in separate orphanages, he traveled toward the northern states. It was revealed at the reunion that Gus fathered an additional fifteen children, by several different women, but never raised any of them. Bill Abner, the only child that kept track of their father, told Mother that Gus died in 1956 in Eldorado, Illinois, where he is now buried.

Mother died on December 18, 1997, never having found her brothers, Carl or Edwin.

Early Life

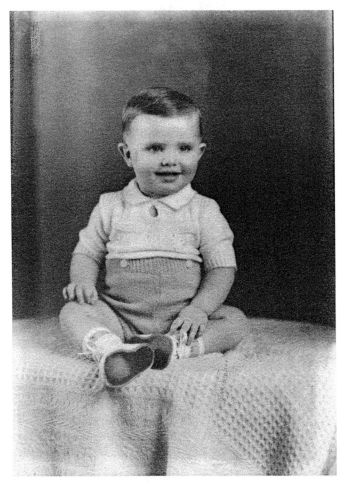

Larry's Baby Picture, 1939

In the Beginning

The house at the corner of Union & Myrtle Streets

Dad and Mom lived for a short time with Grandpa and Grandma Powell after they were married in 1933. Later, they rented their first home, which was located at the southeast corner of Union and Myrtle Streets in Palmyra. Just prior to Roger's birth in 1937, they moved across the street to the southwest corner of Union & Myrtle. Thirteen months later I was born on December 19, 1938. Grandpa, Dr. Powell, delivered both Roger and me at home and I was honored to have been named after Grandpa's & Grandma's deceased son, Harry Lawrence Powell.

The house at the corner of W. Malone & Downing Streets

After Grandpa Mahan died on January 6, 1940, Dad and Mom moved to a larger house, located at the corner of W. Malone and Downing Streets. This move was made to also accommodate Grandma Mahan who moved in with us.

Mooning in Daylight

Roger & Larry, pre-school age 1941

Roger and I were full of vinegar from the git go. What one didn't think of, the other did! The old Palmyra Grade School was located just across the street to the north from our house. The school authorities reported to Dad that Roger and I were seen climbing out onto the porch roof, "mooning" the school kids at recess time. Dad's black belt was all it took to curb that adventure.

Another time, a teacher spotted Roger and me removing boards from the outdoor well. As we were dropping rocks to hear the splash, Mom received a call from the school. Before the end of that week a new well covering had been installed and Dad's belt was getting a workout.

Moving in with Grandpa Powell

Dr. & Mrs. Powell's house on Main Street, 1942

Grandma Powell died on October 16, 1942 and shortly afterward we moved in with Grandpa Powell. Our new home, located on South Main Street, was our second move within five years. Grandma Mahan didn't move with us because she had married Ernest Vancil and moved to Girard, Illinois. Because of limited space in the Powell home, Mom and Dad and Roger had bedrooms upstairs and I slept with Grandpa Powell in the downstairs bedroom. Grandpa had a large jar of horehound candy and he religiously partook of several pieces each night. Between the smell of his candy and his passing of gas (a nightly occurrence), sleeping with Grandpa was a challenge, but I loved it!

Grandpa & Grandma Vancil, 1942

Birth on Blue Ridge

One night in 1944, Grandpa received an urgent telephone call seeking his help to deliver a child. I didn't want to be alone so Grandpa quickly helped me dress and I got to ride "shotgun" in his 1938 Chevy as we headed east of Terry Park. I got to touch the new baby just after birth, which made me feel quite important.

Under Attack

Adults talked about WWII at Dad's shoe and clothing store every day and through listening to various comments, I had developed a fear of war coming to Palmyra. In 1945, when church bells rang and the town siren blew all at the same time, announcing the end of the war, I thought we were under attack. Horrified, I left my little sand box in the front yard and ran all the way to Dad's store. Finding out that the war was over helped, but Dad's loving hug probably had the biggest effect toward soothing a frightened young lad.

A Hand Full

Larry & Roger in elementary school

Whenever Mom and Dad attended their card club or just took a night off (which was seldom), a babysitter was hired to watch the Mahan boys. Marjorie (Powars) Weller, Phyllis (Vance) Kramer, and Maxine (Smith) Zelmer were three of the babysitters that come to mind. Roger and I constantly played pranks on all of them and I'm sure that they more than earned their pay.

Phyllis: Roger and I would wait until Phyllis settled in, either reading a book or listening to the radio. Then, we would go to the back of the living room closet, pull out an old unattached panel, and climb inside. Pulling the panel shut, we would make animal noises or call for help from Phyllis who was in another room. Even though she searched the closet on several occasions, she never found our hiding place. Phyllis was a special person.

Marjorie: There was never a prettier baby sitter than Marjorie Powars, period! She was rather strict and always a step or two ahead of our mischief. On a few occasions, after Roger and I had been put to bed, we heard talking coming from downstairs. Sneaking down we could count on seeing Marvin Pence sitting by her side on the couch. We would yell things like, "we caught you," "kiss her, kiss her," or "wait till we tell Mom and Dad." We never did, though, because Marvin was our hero and Marjorie was our beauty queen.

Maxine: Maxine was the strictest babysitter of all, but she was very fair. She played many games with us right up until bedtime which meant some peace and quiet for her. Later in life, Maxine stated that babysitting the Mahan boys was a challenge she never forgot.

Dad's cousins, the Mahan girls, Marjorie and Carolyn (daughters of Mick and Velma Mahan), were also occasional babysitters. Being cousins, Roger and I limited our many pranks, partially because they kept us busy with outdoor games, snow sledding, and taking walks in the back woods near Ray Pence's house. Sometimes the Harney girls were called upon to watch us. They were beautiful girls, not very strict, and easy to get along with. What fun we had!

Headaches and Heartaches

Christmas Day, 1946, was a difficult day! Grandpa Powell had suffered a major stroke a few months earlier and was in intensive care at the old Carlinville Hospital, located just north of the Macoupin County Court House in Carlinville, Illinois. While Mother was visiting Grandpa, Dad allowed Roger and me to walk uptown on that Sunday afternoon to see the live Gifford Players at the Rockne Theater. On the way home several of us kids were playing tag and as I attempted to jump over a metal fence near Pixley's Variety Store, I was tagged. As I fell I landed on the fence, causing a steel rod to penetrate my brow just above my left eye socket. Truman Holloway noticed that I was crying, with blood streaming down my cheek, so he quickly ran to get Dad, who immediately came to my rescue. Dr. Gauze, another Palmyra doctor, suggested we go see Dr. Sharp in Girard for minor eye surgery. I came home with several stitches and a swollen eye, only to learn that Grandpa Powell had passed away. I felt so sad and so alone!

As so often happens, good things seemed to follow heartaches. One month later Mother gave birth to William Scott Mahan on January 24, 1947 and we were all delighted with this new addition. I was now promoted to my own bed upstairs.

Palmyra Grade School (1944-'50)

Palmyra Grade School

Although I looked forward to my school years, my true love was reading about nature and Indians. When we played Cowboys and Indians at school, I always played the role of an Indian Chief, feather bonnet and all. One year Mom and Dad bought me a velvet Indian vest for my birthday. It was like a dream come true. Thus, it was a major trauma when, in late 1947, Clarence Henry grabbed my vest during recess and tore off a piece of the cotton material. A fight ensued, and even though I got even, my pride and joy always carried a scar despite Mom's best efforts to mend it. As kids most often do, Clarence and I made up quickly and we remained friends all through school.

Larry, Grade 1

The two teachers that I remember the most in grade school were Miss Iva Malone and Mrs. Ivarene Hettick. Due to my lack of interest in academic subjects, especially math and English, I frequently missed recess because of my failure to complete assignments. At the end of my 5th grade year I was passed to the next level on the condition that I complete staggering amounts of English and math worksheets by the end of June. Failure to successfully complete the assignments would result in me being retained. That was the longest June in my life, but I did the work and made sure that it didn't happen again. I learned my lesson and later in life I developed a deep appreciation for both teachers.

Watching the Panthers

One of my thrills during the middle 1940's was going to the Palmyra High School basketball games. At home games a running score was kept on a portable black chalkboard and sometimes I was selected to be the eraser boy as scores were made. I felt like a big shot with a choice seat in that old, very small gym. I still have memories of watching basketball players (stars, to me) such as Marvin Pence, Carrol Cox, Wayne Wiggins, and many other excellent athletes.

Saturday Nights in Palmyra

Rockne Theater, 1937

Saturday nights in Palmyra attracted people from several neighboring communities. Local farmers would often drive their cars to downtown Palmyra in early afternoon to reserve a choice parking spot. During the evening it was quite common to see vehicles full of adults watching people scurrying around town. Most stores were open for business, which included four cafes, five gas stations, three barber shops, and of course, the upscale Rockne Theater, built in 1937.

Hargett's Drug Store, mid 1940s

Hargett's Drug/Novelty Store, two taverns, and Robinson's Pool Hall usually stayed open until late at night.

The dance hall, located above the Spooner Transcript office and the Clover Leaf Grocery Store, attracted dancers from far and wide. Music and dance calls could be heard to the far reaches of town, usually lasting until midnight. The dance hall was off-limits to me, even though every now and then I would sneak up the dark stairs to get a quick look at the action.

Dad's clothing store closed at 9:30 p.m. but there were always a few shoppers that lingered after time. Roger and I were to report to Dad's store at 8:45 p.m. to help empty trash cans and straighten chairs. Dad began turning off lights just after 9:15 p.m. and after the last customer left we would meet Mother at one of the local cafes where she had reserved a table. An ice cream treat was an expected delight, one that we looked forward to. It was not unusual to see the barber shops completely full of customers after 9:30 p.m.

But it Can't Be

One Saturday in 1950 Dad told us that there was going to be a special treat that evening. Evan Richie was going to show off a brand new television in his appliance store window and the broadcast was going to be the Joe Lewis/Ezzard Charles boxing match. Being small, I acquired a front row seat on the sidewalk as a large crowd of adults packed in behind me. As I sat watching the boxing match, my first ever experience watching TV, Dad appeared after 9:30 p.m., kneeling down as he reminded me that I had missed my work chores. He excused my absence, though, as he also watched the ending of the boxing match. Lewis, former heavyweight champion from 1934-'48, was trying to make a comeback against current heavyweight champion Ezzard Charles. Charles won the bout by a unanimous decision and that spelled the end of Joe Lewis' boxing career. Later, I told Dad that I just couldn't believe the fight was live from New York City and that we were watching it on a tiny little box so far away. The exciting new concept of television was simply unbelievable.

Move to the Farm

The Farm

Country Living

Dad enjoyed owning and operating his men's clothing store, but he often talked about his childhood memories of living on a farm five miles east of Palmyra, just north of Blooming Grove Church. Farming was in his blood! Dad's dream of owning his own farm came true in the spring of 1950 when he purchased the Grover Jennings farm located four miles south of Palmyra. The move was made possible partially because Grandpa and Grandma (Mahan) Vancil agreed to buy the Powell house in Palmyra. Mother, who was teaching music in the Northwestern Schools, was not thrilled, to say the least, about our new home. Life on the farm required several immediate changes. Some luxuries that we left in Palmyra were replaced by; a three-holer outhouse, an outdoor pump well, a washtub for Saturday night baths (Roger first, then me in the same water), an oak ice box (electricity came the next year), a four-party phone, and a back bedroom with little heat for Roger and me in the winter. Scott slept nearer the front part of the house where there was more heat.

The barn at the farm

Dad milked ten cows, twice a day, and in season farmed over sixty acres, besides working at his store. Mom performed other farm chores while maintaining her teaching job, and kept a list of jobs for Roger and me after each school day. Before electricity, we used a wooden bucket to store butter and eggs in our twenty five foot deep well. We also made good use of the storm cellar where Mom and Dad stored sugar, salted pork meat, fruit, and garden vegetables.

When electricity was made available, Dad purchased a new set of Sears Surge Milkers, which drastically reduced the milking time. Mom's new electric refrigerator was a life saver for her.

Hot summer nights sometimes forced Roger and me to sleep outside on the ground. Mother made a nice pallet of blankets for our bed and we wrapped ourselves in sheets to ward off the pesky mosquitoes. We would head back to our bed around 2:00 a.m., after the house had cooled down.

Bitter cold nights were also a challenge, but Mom, a great seamstress, was prepared. Previously she had made large tube socks from yarn, just big enough to hold a heated brick. One hour before bedtime, Mom put the warm tube socks under our covers which helped to heat our big feather bed mattress and kept our bed warm for several hours until body heat took over.

When we first moved to the farm, checkers and listening to the big Zenith console radio were our main forms of entertainment. Dad's favorite program was the evening news with Gabriel Heatter. After the news, we often listened to such shows as The Lone Ranger, Hop-a-long Cassidy, Amos and Andy, and, of course, the St. Louis Cardinal ballgames.

In late 1950, Dad and Mom purchased a new television from Richie's appliance store and the tiny, black and white set was an immediate hit. Mom and Dad enjoyed shows like I Love Lucy, Ozzie and Harriet, and The Red Skelton Show, while Howdy Doody was Scott's favorite. Roger and I usually watched The Lone Ranger, Cisco Kid, or Roy Rogers. Having our TV privileges taken away was always a concern, so Roger and I made sure our chores were completed on time.

Our storm cellar was usually full of meats, veggies, and fruit, but on one spring evening the entire family huddled in the cellar as a severe storm approached our farm. The wind was ferocious, causing a large tree to be uprooted. Many limbs and other debris were scattered throughout the yard. The storm cellar served its true purpose that night.

Hettick Grade School

Hettick Grade School, 1950

Roger and I would now be going to grade school in Hettick, two and a half miles to the south of our farm. The four area towns (Hettick, Palmyra, Modesto, and Scottville) consolidated in 1948, which meant that all high school students would go to the old Palmyra high school and each town would retain their own elementary schools, grades 1-8.

Each school day Roger and I walked one quarter of a mile down our lane to State Road 111, where we caught the bus. We discovered that by going early we might get a ride from Mrs. Grace Wiggins and Mr. Henry Brown, our teachers at Hettick, who commuted from Palmyra each day. Even though we felt special being escorted to school, Mr. Brown took advantage of the situation by giving us classroom chores before school began. Sometimes we would finish our chores in time to visit Mrs. Mable Comer, cafeteria cook. She always had a treat for us!

Pass the Gas

Mr. Brown was always full of pranks and jokes which made the school day enjoyable. All except for one! Needing help with a reading assignment, I approached Mr. Brown's desk and as I was standing there, Mr. Brown passed gas with a loud toot. He immediately bellowed, "Larry, shame on you!" The kids all burst out laughing and nothing that I said could convince them that it wasn't me!

The Fire Escape Treat

One day as we were quietly doing our classroom work, Mr. Brown suddenly called us to attention by demanding that we quickly exit the room via the fire escape chute. A little frightened, the class followed Mr. Brown's instructions and in a short time we were all standing on the outside ball field. At that point Mr. Brown told us to look to the south and as we did, an airplane flew overhead, dipping his wings as he passed. We were all thrilled and I could hardly wait until after school to tell Mom and Dad.

Quail Breasts for Arrowheads

Dad bought a used 410 single shot shotgun for my birthday in 1950 and, after much instruction and considerable amounts of learning by trial and error, I was allowed to hunt on my own. I became a decent marksman and because we had an abundance of rabbits and quail on our farm, our freezer remained full of meat. On one occasion Dad told a story about "Dutch" Brown, a resident of Palmyra who had lost a leg due to diabetes. Dad suggested (told me) that we would start providing some of our wild meat for Dutch.

Dad also insisted that the animals be dressed, cleaned, soaked in salt water, and packaged. I thought that was a little much, but Dad reinforced his suggestion by saying, "That's the way it will be, Lawrencie boy." That brought an immediate end to any further objections on my part.

Nassa Creek

Dutch Brown and I became close friends in a short time. I listened intently as he talked about hunting and trapping near Nassa Creek in years past. Then he showed me a box full of Indian relics that he had found in the bottomlands and along the creek. He also displayed some prized artifacts that he had dug from an Indian mound. My passion for Indian lore soared! Later, he provided a hand drawn map directing me to certain locations near our farm where artifacts could be found. I made sure to visit Dutch at least every other week, trading wild game for stories about other artifact areas, including those along Solomon Creek. Those visits were priceless!

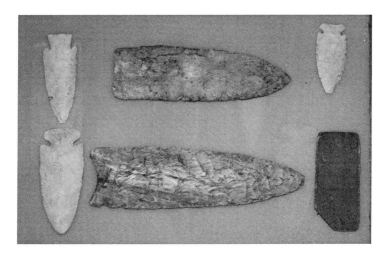

Indian Artifact Collection

First Things First

During the summer and on Saturdays during the school year, I eagerly awaited my free time. First of all I had to tend to my assigned chores such as; cleaning the chicken coop and gathering eggs, cleaning the milking stalls in the barn, and keeping the yard mowed. Also, Roger and I were required to pick up a certain amount of rocks from the old abandoned railroad (closed in 1941) that traversed through our farm. We were able to fill up several washed out ditches with our labors. After my chores were completed, Mom would make a couple of peanut butter sandwiches, plus fruit from our cellar, and I was off to Nassa Creek. Water was no problem as I drank from ripple areas in the creek. My only instruction was to be home by 4:00 p.m. to begin my chores all over again.

Turtle Treat

Harold & Nellie Maguire, 1949

At Hettick Junior High School I quickly made friends with Pete Maguire. Pete, and his dad, Harold, also collected Indian relics that they found near Nassa Creek, just west of our farm. Pete's parents, Harold and Nellie, were very kind and their house became my home away from home. During one meal, Nellie asked how I liked the meat, and I stated that it was the best beef I had ever eaten. That's when Nellie said, "Larry, this is turtle meat." I couldn't believe that it tasted so good as I asked for seconds.

Several times on my one and a half mile walk to the Maguire farm I would run into Jack Mitch or Donnie Cochran. They were either doing farm work in the bottomland or, to my surprise, looking for arrowheads. They directed me to other areas where flint and artifacts could be found. I will always remember their kindness.

Dangerous Shortcut

On one occasion, during spring flooding, I was running late and hurrying toward home from the Maguire farm. When Dad said to be home by 4:00 p.m. that is exactly what he meant and being late was not acceptable. Penalties would result. Realizing that I would probably be late, I remembered a steel cable that crossed the creek from tree to tree. Instead of walking another few hundred yards to the abandoned steel bridge (passable only by foot), I decided to 'walk' hand and feet across the cable. The creek was bank full as I held on for dear life only a couple of feet above the fast moving water. The cable was quite old and splintery and by the time I reached the other side my hands and ankles were bleeding. I rushed to the barn just in the nick of time for evening chores. Dad asked about my hands and I made up some wild story about a barbed wire fence.

The Cigar Story

For a change, I would sometimes head north on Nassa Creek and visit the Richie family (boys-Waldo, Wendall, & Larry) or to play with Carl Weller. On one occasion, Carl and I were sitting in his brother's old Ford car, pretending to be driving. I found an old cigar in the side panel and thought it would be "cool" to chew it. After swallowing some of the cigar juice, I suddenly became quite ill. I hurried to a near- by fence and threw up the brine and all my lunch. As I supported myself on the fence, I saw something on the ground and yelled to Carl, "Look, there's an arrowhead." Even today, it is one of my prized arrowheads.

The Raccoon Family

Just across Nassa Creek, on the side of a hill, was a wide spreading white oak tree. One of the limbs drooped almost to the ground and I noticed a den hole in the trunk with feces scattered around the limb. As I quietly sat on the ground, a tiny raccoon emerged from the den, followed by other siblings. Over a period of several weeks, after leaving treats of apples, the raccoons became somewhat friendly. The young coons would scamper down the limb when they heard me coming and wait, two to three feet away, as I put treats on the branch. They would stay there until I retreated, and then the entire family would dine on the treats. Although I never touched any of them, their chatter as I approached let me know that they appreciated my gifts.

Postscript: Many years later loggers cut down the "coon tree" for a mere nine foot log. How sad!

Pig Delivery

In addition to his dairy herd, Dad also raised a few swine for butchering purposes. On one afternoon, Dad asked me to come to the birthing cage where an older sow was having great difficulty trying to deliver her litter of pigs. Dad greased my right arm with lard and then instructed me as to my next step in delivering the piglets. The sow was lying down, not far from death, as I inserted my arm into her womb. Immediately I felt a body turned sideways. With a little straightening I was able to remove the dead pig, followed by another dead sibling. The other births were much easier, followed by the normal afterbirth. Eventually the mother pig regained her strength, but in the meantime, we had to bottle feed the surviving piglets. Dad rewarded my help by giving me one of the litter and I felt good about my life saving efforts.

The Rumble and the Roar

Freddie Passalacqua and his midget race car

One of my special treats in the late 1940s and early 1950s was attending the midget car races just north of Hettick, Illinois. Dad liked to watch the races, so we were frequent visitors to the racetrack, located one mile south of our farm. Some of the local drivers included Tink McCaherty, Chuck Jennings, Pinky Shinpaugh, Cyril Solomon and Freddie Passalacqua. I always rooted for Freddie because on a few occasions he let me sit in his classy black car.

1951-A Year of Trauma

Mom and Dad and we three boys drove to Springfield, Illinois on Sunday, May 27, 1951 to visit Wendell, Clara, and Jeffrey Hoover. Little did we realize that our lives, on that Sunday, would take a dramatic change.

Just after our Sunday meal with the Hoovers, Dad received a phone call from his mother, frantically telling him to hurry home because the town was burning down. We left in a hurry and along the way were stopped by the Auburn police for speeding. When Dad informed the policeman of the disaster in Palmyra, he let us continue without issuing a speeding ticket.

From Waverly, Illinois we could see the smoke rising in the sky, some eleven miles away. At the north edge of Palmyra, we could see the enormous fire almost a mile away. We parked two blocks from downtown Palmyra and quickly ran toward the intersection. As we approached the downtown area, Dad's store caved in with a loud roar. The total damage was beyond belief. More than ten businesses were destroyed. This was one of the few times that I saw my dad become emotional.

1951 Palmyra fire, looking east on State Street

May 27, 1951, Palmyra fire, looking south on Main Street

Other businesses destroyed included: Robinson Restaurant; the Post Office; Carl Robinson Pool Hall; the Palmyra Transcript; Chase Variety Store; O'Neal's Novelty Store; Steinmetz Red & White Grocery; M. Steinmetz Second-Hand Store; Ross Insurance; K.P. Hall; the Masonic Hall; the Dance Hall. Nothing was salvaged from Dad's store and, to make matters worse, he had little insurance on the building or the contents. Also, his huge metal safe proved to be not "safe" at all. The safe contained money from the previous week, plus mementoes that were invaluable; a letter from the St. Louis Cardinals inviting him to attend a tryout for a minor league baseball team, and a pair of socks that belonged to Robert Wadlow, the Alton, Illinois Giant, who grew to 8'11 ¼" in height, with a shoe size of 37AA. Dad and Mom were devastated, to say the least, and our future was anyone's guess.

Robert Wadlow, age 12, his brother, Eugene, age 6, and
Harold Shipley, age 5

As we were sifting through the burned remains the next day, I wandered next door to the burned out O'Neil Variety (gambling) Store. While sorting through the debris, I found a rounded metal tube with lots of weight and took it home; not knowing what was in the tube. Within the next day or so, Dad observed me playing with the tube and after he broke open one end, quarters spilled out on the ground. Dad told me that the tube was from one of Peck O'Neil's slot machines. I shouted with joy, thinking I was rich, but Dad, ready to instill another lesson of life, told me that the quarters weren't mine and that we would return them to Peck. Mr. O'Neil was very pleased with my honesty and gave me a $5.00 reward. As we drove home, though, I felt good about doing the right thing.

The next few weeks were decision time for Mom and Dad. Dad loved the farm life but missed the clothing store and his loyal customers. Mom, equally devastated, urged Dad to think about re-opening another store. Now that I look back, I think Mom could visualize a move back to Palmyra. In late summer of 1951, the O.J. Miller store building, just east of Dad's demolished store, was offered for sale. Dad thought the price was affordable, so with Mother teaching school and with another bank loan, Mahan's Clothing Store opened again in the fall of 1952.

Then, on October 25, 1951, Grandma (Mahan) Vancil suddenly passed away leaving Grandpa Vancil very lonely. Grandpa soon decided to move to a smaller home with less upkeep and responsibilities. With the hope of moving back to Palmyra, Mom urged Dad to put our farm up for sale and re-purchase the Powell house from Grandpa Vancil. A buyer for the farm was quickly found and by the summer of 1952 we were back in Palmyra. Leaving the farm left me heartbroken and somewhat bitter, a feeling that stayed with me for years to come.

Back
to
Palmyra

Aerial street scene of Palmyra Centennial Celebration, 1955

The Lure of Nassa Creek

After moving back to Palmyra, I continued to visit Dutch Brown, swapping wild game for friendship and more stories concerning Indian artifact locations. Frequently I would ride my bike on the Russell Gordon/Rollin Giller/ Wayne King road, all the way to the bridge on Nassa Creek, just west of Alfred Weller's farm. From there, I would walk down and back, following Nassa Creek to our old farm place. I frequently found a nice arrowhead or two and also continued to visit the old white oak tree with new litters of coons.

Do's and Don't's

Dad and Mom gave us three boys plenty of latitude as far as discovery and trying new things. Minor errors were always acceptable! However, Dad's basic demands that could never be compromised were:

1. Never talk back or be rude to your mother.
2. Always be respectful of old people, young children, and minority cultures.
3. Visit our neighborhood's older people on a regular basis. (Those people included Zula Duncan, Bill Flenchie, Hat Need, Sam Chase, Mrs. Linder, Ralph and Euna Boyer.
4. No tobacco or alcohol-period!

Zula Duncan House

Mother supported Dad's basic rules but would, on occasion, negotiate our lack of performance for household favors. Mom was known for her meals and treats for the elderly people and she was quick to volunteer, chauffeuring her lady friends on shopping trips, to doctor appointments, and to the St. Louis Municipal Opera. Mom had a big heart!

Sunday Morning Sidewalks

During good weather, Sunday morning sidewalks were active as many people walked to the church of their choice. That was probably a good thing as most church parking lots were full, especially as more and more rural churches closed. The town churches that served our immediate area were; Catholic, Baptist, Methodist, Christian, and Apostolic.

Palmyra Christian Church, 1923

I was baptized at age twelve at the Palmyra Christian Church, where we regularly attended. Mother played the piano for church and Roger, Scott, and I sat with our parents. Finding five seats in the rear of the church was generally not a problem because Dad was a stickler for arriving early. I always pitied the late arrivals as the only seats available were located right down front.

Curt Giller and I frequently volunteered to take the communion trays to the basement after church. We were praised for our efforts, although our ulterior motive was to finish off the grape juice and the yeast bread squares.

On occasion I also attended the Methodist Church to sit by a special girl who attended there.

No Idle Time

Soon after moving back to Palmyra, Dad bought two push mowers (no motor) for Roger and me. We quickly scoured the area for yards to mow, which averaged from $1.00-$2.00 per yard. George Lobb kept our reels (round mower blades) sharpened in return for mowing his large lawn.

In late spring Dad would take us to a grove of sassafras trees and we would dig roots that people used for tea. Small bundles of from fifteen to twenty three inch roots (sticks) were sold to eager customers for twenty five cents and we always had standing orders from several people.

In winter time, when possible, we shoveled snow with special snow shovels that Dad bought for us. Our asking price was twenty five to fifty cents per walkway, but many people paid us more. Dad gave us a list of people who were to have their walks shoveled for free.

In late summer/early fall, we would load up in Dad's old 1946 Chevy slant back and head to Gish's Melon Farm near Beardstown, Illinois. We would fill the car full of watermelons and cantaloupes for a certain set price, and then bring them home to sell at a stand located at our house. With prices of twenty five cents for cantaloupes and fifty to seventy five cents for watermelons, we quickly sold our entire stock.

Later, Roger and I became the "paper boys" for the Springfield, Illinois Journal/Register. We both had bikes equipped with a large metal basket attached to the handle bars and the front wheel. At 6:00 a.m. each morning we would arrive at Bramley's Cafe where stacks of the Illinois State Journal had been delivered. We folded each paper into a flattened parcel, loaded our bike baskets, and set off on our routes. Roger delivered papers to the east side of town, while I serviced the west side. After we finished our routes we met back at Bramley's Café for sausage gravy on a huge, fresh biscuit, plus juice to drink. When the weather turned cold, Mrs. Bramley began serving us coffee, but we told her that Dad didn't allow us to drink coffee. Mrs. Bramley said emphatically, "Any child that gets out this early to deliver papers deserves to drink coffee to warm you up!" After we finished our first ever cup of coffee (with plenty of cream and sugar), Mrs. Bramley told us that she would talk to Dad that very same day. True to her word, later that evening, Dad told us that Mrs. Bramley had visited his store and he guessed we were old enough to have one cup of coffee per day, only if we were delivering newspapers. Virgie Bramley was our hero and a good friend from then on.

In late fall, after corn fields had been harvested, Roger and I would pick up leftover ears of corn on the halves for area farmers. We would walk the corn rows and throw the ears in piles. At the end of the day we would load the piles of corn onto a truck or wagon. Once the corn had been delivered to the local elevator, our half share of money was divided between Roger and me. It was back breaking work but we usually made good money.

Saturday morning at Mahan's Clothing Store. L-R: Buster Bristow, Lester J. Cox, Rollin Giller, Harry Crawford, Paul Mahan, Wesley Jett.

When we were not working elsewhere on Saturdays, Dad expected one of us to work at the store for a couple of hours. Our jobs included sweeping the wooden floor and carrying several loads of trash to the burn barrel located in a vacant lot behind Dad's store. There was a steady flow of customers on Saturdays but there were also selected groups of men who gathered around the Zeigler heating stove, swapping stories about farming, biggest and best things, sports, memory quizzes, hunting, etc. Some of the regulars included Wesley Jett, Adam Fetter, Lester Cox, Buster Bristow, Melvin Bettis, Ray Keller, Ray Pence, Rollin Giller, Art Runyon, and others.

Paul inside his shoe and clothing store, 1958

Dad didn't allow us to join in the conversations because, as to him, it was not proper. One day the men were discussing large trees but couldn't recall where a big sassafras tree was located. One of the men mentioned that he knew where one was growing that was as big around as his thigh. Without thinking, I spoke up and said that I knew where a much bigger one was located. Adam Fetter, testing my knowledge, questioned me about the shape of leaves. I told him that sassafras trees had three different shape leaves and with that, he wanted to know how big this tree was. "It is bigger than your waist, Adam," I said, causing all the other men to laugh because Adam had a huge stomach. Adam asked me to take him to the tree in question. Later that day, Adam and I walked along Solomon Creek bottomland and as I pointed out the huge sassafras, Adam remarked to me, "Little Larry, your sassafras is the biggest that I have ever seen." Later, Adam shared our venture with the locals at Dad's store and I felt ten feet tall. Dad was even pleased with the news, even though I knew that I had to continue to be just a listener.

Where's the Institution?

On one particular Saturday, a salesman walked into Dad's store, smiling and shaking his head. Dad could sense a good story as he asked the salesman what was funny. The salesman asked Dad if our little town had a mental institution. He went on to say that the five men, (Polk Stewart, Harley Shinpaugh, Chick Chase, Griz Huson, and Shorty Brannen)who were sitting on the store's front ledge were jabbering and arguing with each other and when he asked them a question each of the men all talked at once, without ever answering the question. Dad told the salesman that they were "our leading citizens." That brought about a head shaking laugh, but Dad didn't mean his words to be a put down or cruel. Less fortunate people held a special place in Dad's heart.

Secret Santa

One Christmas Eve during the early 1950s as I was returning home from caroling, I noticed that the trunk on Dad's old Chevy was slightly ajar. I walked to the car and raised the trunk lid and to my surprise I noticed a trunk full of packages. Each package was labelled with penciled initials, such as 'FR' on the flap side, so it couldn't be easily seen. When I walked into the house I told Dad what I had seen. He quickly stood up and rushed me towards the kitchen, where he quietly began telling me the story. For several years on Christmas Eve, Dad would deliver his anonymous clothing gifts to those in need. Late at night he would drive the darkened streets in town, slipping the gifts inside the screen doors (very few people locked their doors then) or on the front car seat. Because of farm dogs, certain rural deliveries required using the mailbox for delivery. Dad's words to me were simple and strong, "You are not to tell anyone about what you saw," "It is our secret!" And I didn't, until years later after Dad passed away.

Calling on the Elderly

Dad made it a point to check on our expected visits to the neighborhood elderly people. Not having enough time was never an acceptable excuse! I did, however, enjoy most of the many visits as I learned a lot about "olden times" from early settler days, the Civil War, the depression, WWI, WWII, and the good times that followed. Of all of my visits, the ones that I seem to cherish the most were those with ninety six year old Mrs. Emma Linder. Not only was she mentally alert, she was also eager to share her information. I was aghast when she mentioned, as a young ten year old girl, seeing several Civil War veterans walking home after the war. She mentioned their worn out boots, their knapsacks, and their guns. They caught rides on trains heading north when possible, walking again as they received food and shelter from Union sympathizers. They were the heroes of Palmyra, she remembered, as well as those who came later following WWI, WWII, and the Korean conflict.

Saturday Nights after the 1951 Fire

The entire southwest block of Martin Buildings was destroyed by the 1951 fire, but within a few months plans were made to build a new bank at the southwest corner of Main and State Streets. The new bank was completed in September, 1952. Other businesses that followed were the U.S. Post Office, Palmyra Café, and Eyer's Electric Shop. Mahan's Clothing Store relocated just east of the burned out vacant lot, to the vacant O.J. Miller Plumbing/Hardware Store in the fall of 1952. Dad's store was open for business again!

Unfortunately, Saturday nights were never quite the same after the horrible fire in 1951. Local people were forced to shop for groceries, clothing, and other necessities at neighboring towns and while out of town they also spent money for gas, food, and entertainment. Carlinville's new Diane Drive In, which opened in 1952, became a popular attraction for young couples and eating at Taylor's Chili was considered a special treat. England's Drive-In, Hettick,

Illinois, attracted people from all four Northwestern towns as they savored the burgers, fries, and hand dipped milkshakes.

The Diane Drive-In movie theater, 1952

With the advent and availability of television, many people chose to stay home and watch their favorite TV programs. 'People watching' in downtown Palmyra became a thing of the past.

Early High School Years

Modesto High School

I attended Hettick Grade School for seventh and eighth grades and after moving back to Palmyra from the farm, I was ready for high school. Since consolidation in 1948, each community (Hettick, Palmyra, Modesto, and Scottville) housed their own grade school students. Because of lack of space at the Northwestern High School in Palmyra, the ninth graders from all four communities went to school at Modesto. In 1953, I started my sophomore year at the Northwestern High School in Palmyra. I usually walked to school, taking short cuts through yards so as to lessen my five minute walk.

Northwestern High School

After School Treats

On days when I wasn't required to come right home, I would often make a quick stop at one of the following places:

1. Bristow's Garage. Mrs. Bristow was known far and wide for selling huge carmel apples. For ten cents a person could buy a heavenly treat.

2. Scrim Scroggins Shell Station. During my extra time I would ride around town all the way to the edge, looking for soda pop bottles that people would discard. Scrim paid one cent per bottle for returns and he kept track of how many I turned in during the week. I could usually count on enough credits to partake of an Orange Crush and a Snicker's bar every other week. Scrim was such a friend to all the kids as he fixed flats on their bikes and repaired spokes in wheels for free. He was always giving advice about helping the less fortunate. What a role model!

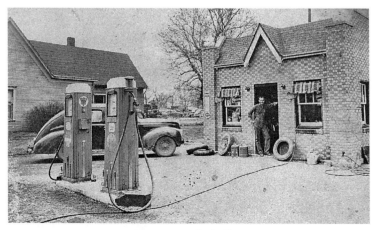

Scrim Scroggins' Shell Station

3. The Luttrell home. Kids were always welcome to go to Red and Lola Luttrell's house after school. Along with their son, Gene, we played ping pong and checkers in the basement for an hour or so. Then, Lola served Kool-Ade and cookies as a special treat before we left for home. Lola kept tabs on our activities and we always knew the limits to our behaviors.

Free Shows

In the early 1950s, the four area communities hired Russell "Whistle" Eyer to show movies at their outdoor City Parks. With a huge screen and a modern projector, Whistle presented a wide array of films such as the ever popular Zorro series. Whistle also sold popcorn from his Chevy van.

Parents would take their children to a grassy location and then shop at the various stores surrounding the park. It was not uncommon to see over one hundred kids of all ages huddled together on individual blankets in anticipation of watching their favorite programs. It was also a special time for young couples (boyfriend/girlfriend) to share a sack of popcorn as they cuddled together. With Dad and Mom's permission, I often accompanied Whistle to various towns, helping him "set up" for the evening show. For my reward, I was afforded all the popcorn that I could eat.

Carrying the Sack

Adam Fetter with the catfish he caught by hand fishing

A popular outdoor activity in the summer time was hand fishing (also called 'logging'). Dad and some of his friends would locate deep water holes in area creeks that had been formed because of submerged logs. The men would swim beneath the water and under the logs to 'feel' for trapped carp and catfish. Attached hand hooks were sometimes used to catch the fish but most often the men would just use their hands as they grabbed the fish inside its mouth. The pleasure of bringing to shore a two to three pound fish seemed to outweigh the pain of the scrapes and hand cuts that were common. Because I was too jumpy, I seldom caught any fish, so I was demoted to carrying the gunny sack which held the day's catch. Usually a big fish fry followed our successful outing and many of Mom and Dad's older friends were invited to our feast.

Talley Ho

On warm Saturday nights, when we were out of spending money, or wanted a different challenge, several of us boys would play a game that we developed, called 'talley ho'. After two teams were chosen, one team would take off, either on foot or on a bicycle, yelling "talley ho" as they passed street intersections throughout town. Team number two waited for one minute and then started the chase, trying to catch and tag someone from the running team. As soon as kids were tagged they joined in the hunt for the remaining runners. We learned rather quickly as we chose sides, to pick not only the fastest partners but also those with endurance. The object of our game was to sneak back to home base without being caught (tagged). Scores were kept and honesty was sometimes questioned, causing some players to be excluded from other adventures.

Fish and Ice Cream

Driving to Kampsville, Illinois to eat fish was always a treat for our family. We three boys could hardly wait until we were aboard the Kampsville Ferry watching the little tug boat move us to the other side. Dad pointed out the huge cable that helped secure our safe ride as we crossed the Illinois River. Roger and I sometimes would tease Scott about the cable breaking. Several family members made the trip together, buying fresh carp and catfish at a local market upon reaching the other side. The adults would cook our fish at the City Park or at Pere Marquette State Park, and share side dishes that they had brought, as we all enjoyed a great feast.

Paul making ice cream

Sunday afternoons were special times in most small towns, as families would often rotate visiting in each other's homes. Kids loved the get-togethers as it meant playing ball, croquet, and other yard games. The big highlight, of course, was the making of homemade ice cream. When friends came to our home, Dad took pride in having the biggest White Mountain freezer around. My brother, Scott, was often given the first round of hand cranking, which made him feel extra special.

Going Nowhere…

Carl Robinson's pool hall was a popular hangout for kids and adults alike. Men played cards (gambled) in the backroom while pool players and loafers stayed in the larger front area. Carl was easy to get along with until he began drinking, and then look out! Sometimes kids would tease Carl by hiding his chair, barking like a dog, switching off the lights, etc. just to see Mr. Robinson's reactions. Carl walked with a severe limp, so his movements were limited, and with enough alcohol consumption his handicap became more evident. I didn't like to see people take advantage of Carl, so when problems started to develop, I generally went outside and sat on a store front ledge until things quieted down. One evening as I was sitting on Dad's store front ledge, several older boys put a cement block under Johnny Eyer's 'Model A' Ford car, so that the rear wheels barely touched the ground. When Johnny entered his car to go home, his car wouldn't move and after several attempts, he looked under his car and saw the block under the rear wheel axle. Johnny was quite mad and after help arrived to remove the block, he left cussing up a storm.

Another such incident had a more pleasing ending. Shorty Brannen owned a tiny two-door Crosley sedan car that he often parked just west of the pool hall. One night after Shorty entered the poolroom, four boys picked up his little Crosley car and turned it around, 180°. When Shorty came out to go home, he walked around to the street side of his car, only to realize that the door opened the wrong way. Shorty, an older gentleman with a warm personality, walked around his car several times, shaking his head, before he finally figured out what had happened. With a big smile, he started his car and drove off, saying, "You guys!" Shorty was a good sport and a friend to everyone.

Down the Air-Vent Pipe

I often heard stories of late night activities that were going on at the two local taverns and, of course, Hargett's Drug Store. One Friday night in 1952, after Mom and Dad had gone to bed, I climbed out the upstairs bedroom onto the back porch roof, shimmied down the sewer air-vent pipe, and headed downtown. Because of the dim street lights, it was very dark between the intersections, so I jogged the four block distance in a hurry. I would never dream of hanging around the taverns, so I went to Hargett's Drug Store and sat on the outside ledge, watching people come and go. Several couples were coming and going, and it seemed like everyone was smoking cigarettes. Most people didn't acknowledge my presence, probably because I sat off to one side. I quickly learned some new phrases that I assumed were not to be repeated, such as "piece of tail." I was young for my age and didn't fully understand some of the eye opening comments.

After my second visit to Hargett's Drug Store, two young men approached me and said, "Hey, little Shorty, you better hope that Paul doesn't find out that you are sneaking out of the house this late at night." As I hurried home, I knew that I would not be going back.

Me and My Bike

I loved my bicycle and during my free moments I often took off on different routes. When I ventured southwest, I generally rode to Melvin or Freddie Bettis' farm, stopping long enough to savor welcomed treats and hear stories and funny jokes. I can still remember some of Melvin's "Febbie" jokes and seeing all the Freddie Bettis kids enjoying life to its fullest. These were two of my favorite stops. On the way home I often detoured to Solomon Creek and looked for arrowheads on sand bars. My other favorite bike rides started at the south edge of Palmyra along the Russell Gordon farm. From there I would ride past Rollin Giller's farm, past Wayne King's home, (both great water break stops), and then on south to the bridge over Nassa Creek. I would then walk down Nassa Creek bottomland looking for Indian artifacts, of course. By the time I arrived back home I had covered approximately seven miles, usually returning with a couple of new arrowheads.

Arrowhead Collection

Who's There?

Telephone pranks became popular during the 1950s, and as usual, some of us were often the instigators. We often targeted grocery stores, asking such questions as, "Do you have Old Judge (coffee) in a can?", "Does Aunt Jemima come in a box?",etc. When the answer was yes, our reply would be, "You better turn him/her loose before they suffocate." Our little games ended as word got out and especially after Gaby Shearburn replied, "We just turned him/her loose today," followed by his robust laugh.

One Sunday afternoon when Mom and Dad were gone, we noticed that Mr. and Mrs. David Gates were having an outdoor gathering in their yard for school teachers. We could easily see the party from our house and when everyone sat down for afternoon treats, we telephoned the Gates residence. As soon as Mr. Gates entered the back door, we hung up the phone. Then, a few minutes later, we pulled the same prank again. We waited a little longer for our next call but just before we started dialing, Mr. Cox, our high school principal entered our back door, announcing that our little gig was over. He emphatically stated that any further calls would be reported to Dad. Needless to say, our little game was over-Mr. (Sly Fox) Cox made sure of that!

In the Outhouse

Most of the time during Halloween, kids dressed up in various costumes, hoping to fool our friends and neighbors, resulting in extra candy. Sometimes Halloween fostered pranks, such as overturning outhouses. Lowell Hughes' outhouse was considered a challenge as he would hide on his back porch, ready at a moment's notice to yell or chase us. I remember one night when we were sneaking up to "dump" the shanty, Lowell was hiding in it. As we approached, he cursed and began chasing us. We ran between houses and I failed to see a clothesline, which caught me by the neck. I fell to the ground, stunned and out of breath, but I stayed very still, hoping Lowell would not see me. As luck would have it, and with the help of the poorly lighted street lights, Lowell ran past me, cursing to "who laid it!"

We told some older boys about our scary encounter and they came up with a perfect plan. After constructing a board with nails at both ends, the guys hid at night, waiting within eyesight of the Hughes outhouse. After a couple of nights with no luck, they finally caught a glimpse of Mr. Hughes heading towards the outhouse, ready for invaders. Three boys, quietly sneaking towards the outhouse, placed the board on the entrance side and quickly nailed the door shut. As some of us kids watched from a distance, we could hear Mr. Hughes cursing, using all kinds of bad words. Later, I heard some adults talking in Dad's store, saying that Lowell had bought some shotgun shells to use if it didn't stop. Dad, not knowing of my involvement, told me to stay away from that side of town. I did!

Terry Park Fairs

The highlight of each year was the three day Terry Park Fair. Mayor Oral Cooper first acquired a top notch carnival company that featured several up-to-date rides, fast food stands, and two or more side shows. Mayor Cooper worked day and night organizing hobby/craft displays, talent shows, and the ever popular community food building.

The Fair attracted huge crowds from several surrounding communities.

Tent Peeking

The tent shows drew large crowds, but they were strictly for adults. That didn't stop some of us kids, though, from peeking under the tent on the dark back side. During one fair I got my first look at a nude woman. What a sight!

The Wild Animal Man

Another tent attraction that lasted only one night was the long haired wild man that dressed in animal skins. He would entertain packed crowds for his twenty minute exhibition as he devoured heads from live chickens and then held the carcasses above his head and drank the blood that drained. For his finale he would put two live small snakes in his mouth and then let them crawl in and around his head. After many complaints, the Wild Man tent show was closed.

Blue Ribbons at Terry Park

Whenever I had free time I often went back to Nassa Creek, looking for Indian artifacts and checking on the White Oak coon tree. My artifact collection represented many years of labor and I was quite proud of my endeavors. Several times I entered my collection in the Terry Park Hobby Contest and each time I received a blue ribbon. It was then that I remembered Dutch Brown, Jack Mitch, Donnie Cochran, and Harold & Pete Maguire. It was due to their guidance I became familiar with great locations near Nassa Creek in my quest for finding Indian artifacts.

Arrowhead Collection

Taking Jap Home

Mom and Dad owned two cars and the newer car was the one that Mom drove to the four Northwestern elementary schools where she taught music. Dad's car was an older 1946 slant back Chevy, one that was used as his hunting car and for all kinds of hauling projects. Dad walked to his clothing store on good weather days, always eager to stay in shape. On a few Saturday occasions when Mom was gone, I took Dad's car for a spin, even though I lacked a driver's license. Jap Rogers lived south and east of Palmyra, nearly five miles from town. He usually walked to town on Saturdays to grocery shop for the next week, but he always made his last stop at one of the local taverns. Heading home in late afternoon, Jap could be seen carrying a large white feed sack full of groceries as he looked for a ride to Richie Road, some three miles south of Palmyra. On one particular Saturday, as Jap walked by our house, I offered him a ride, and as usual, he was elated. I delivered Mr. Rogers to his home and began my trip back to Palmyra. I hadn't traveled far when I met a county police car. As I looked back he began turning around, so I quickly turned north onto a side road with dust flying, and continued to a seldom used back road. I could see the policeman in my rear view mirror as I crossed a farmer's wood plank bridge spanning a small stream. On the other side of the make-shift bridge, I jumped out and removed two planks from one side and then sped on just out of the pursuing policeman's sight. As quick as I could I hurried home, parking Dad's car in the garage and closing the old wooden doors. Later, as I hid and watched from inside our home, I spotted the county police car cruising the streets in town, looking for an old slant back car. Somehow, I dodged the bullet!

A Missed Curve

Another time, but with different results, I decided to take Dad's car to go see a girl that I was trying to impress. I had driven a little over a mile southeast from Palmyra where, going too fast, I wrecked Dad's car on the Zelmer curve. Low and behold, just after I wrecked Dad's car, Mrs. Zelmer and her daughters walked up to the curve, trying to console me in my obvious distress. Even though the damage was minor, I knew that Dad would be very upset. To my surprise, after a "talking to," Dad forgave my error in judgment, but with a stern warning. He also never left his keys in the car again.

A Winner on #9 at Terry Park

Although I enjoyed playing pick-up softball games and tag football, I never was that much interested or athletically inclined to play organized sports. Dad thought that I possessed talent for playing golf, and with his coaching and support I began playing golf at Terry Park on a frequent basis. By 1953 my golf game had improved to the point that I entered the Terry Park Golf Tournament for the fifteen to sixteen year old age bracket. Clarence Henry was an excellent golfer and I felt elated that we were tied at the end of the eighth hole. Tensions mounted as we teed off on the final hole, across the pond to #9 green. Both our tee shots landed on the green but I sank a critical putt for the victory. As the winner, I was rewarded with six new golf balls and a metal tray that had been hand-painted by Kathryn Bramley.

First Prize/1953 Golf Tournament

The Bramleys at Terry Park, early 1950s

Sunday Night Specials

Mom was an excellent cook. Her pies and cakes always received positive reviews at social gatherings. However, on Sunday nights it was Dad's turn to share his favorites. Popcorn (the old fashioned way) and apples from the basement storeroom was Dad's favorite snack. For a change, Dad would concoct a large skillet of fried potatoes (including the skins) along with onions and peppers and fry the ingredients in lard until the potatoes were a crisp, golden brown. Yummy! In the winter time, a glass of cider from the fifty gallon barrel located just outside the house, added to our perfect treat. In late winter, the few remaining gallons of cider developed quite a "kick". That's when Dad really enjoyed his cider!

Red Ryder Rides Again

One Saturday evening as I was cleaning the store for Dad, someone entered the front door, loudly proclaiming that an odd looking man was parked across the street. We looked out the showcase window and observed a tall man sitting in a convertible jeep, just across the street from Dad's store. After receiving Dad's permission, I ran across the street and watched in amazement as the 6'5" man, with long hair and sideburns to match, stepped out of his jeep. Close up I noticed his huge ear rings and a smaller ring protruding from his nose. John Tipton, the intriguing looking giant of a man, had recently been engaged to marry Lorraine Clevenger. Lorraine and her mother operated Mom's Café, located on the west side of South Main Street. John became "a fixture" around town, often telling stories about riding horses in the Girard, Illinois area. Henceforth, John became known as "Red Ryder," a title that he did not appreciate. John gave special attention to the younger generation as we frequently visited with him at Mom's Café. Dad said not to believe all of John's stories.

New Neighbors

Just after the 1953 school year had ended, a new family moved to Palmyra, only two blocks from the Mahan home. Almost immediately Jimmy Scantling and I became best friends. After our daily summer chores/work was finished, Jimmy and I were often seen together on our bikes or with a fishing pole headed towards ponds near town.

Lesson Learned

Once, when I borrowed Dad's car, I drove to the Scantling home to pick up Jimmy. As we started to leave, Jimmy's little brother, Alton, who wanted to go with us, grabbed onto the driver's side door. As I speeded up he let go, but the rear tire slightly pinched his toe. Alton screamed as he ran into the house so we stopped to see what was wrong. I felt bad after seeing his bleeding little toe as Jimmy and I soaked his foot in cold water. Just as we finished tending to Alton, Mr. Scantling came home from delivering coal and boy, did he get mad! He told us that even though Alton shouldn't have grabbed hold of the car door, we were the older, responsible ones and should not have driven off with Alton hanging on for dear life. Then, Mr. Scantling reinforced what we knew to be true by saying, "You, Larry, shouldn't be driving your Dad's car anyway. I won't tell on you this time but from now on, be more careful!" I agreed and thanked Mr. Scantling.

The Moving Purse

In our spare time, Jimmy and I were constantly thinking of ways to have fun. We never considered destroying property or hurting someone or making fun of people. We just wanted to create laughter. One afternoon we took one of Mom's old purses, glued monopoly dollar bills on the outside, and tied a fishing line to the purse. We located ourselves on the curve at the north edge of town, near a road culvert. We placed the purse near the road (Rt. 111), hid in the culvert, and waited for cars to stop to collect their prize. If anyone approached the purse, we would quickly reel in the line. Some people just laughed, while others cursed at us.

The best result of all was when Dorothy Schramm stopped and slowly walked back to the purse. As she reached down to grab it, we gently jerked the line, moving the purse a few inches. Mrs. Schramm yelped, jumped, and looked all around, before reaching for the purse a second time. Again we jerked the line, moving the purse even farther. As we stood up, giggling, Mrs. Schramm burst into laughter and said, "I might have known it was you two kids." She was a good sport. She often told that story in later years.

Our little game came to a quick halt, though, after a state policeman observed us as we were replacing the purse by the road. We ran and hid in the culvert and didn't come out at his command. He finally gave up and drove off. No more purse games for us as the word got around town pretty quick. Dad made sure of that!

The culvert that saved us from the policeman

Beardstown on a Sunday

Before Jimmy and I were old enough to drive, we were constantly looking for a chance to get out of town. Norman and Loren Vance frequently made trips to Beardstown in the fall to buy watermelons and sometimes they would ask Jimmy and me to tag along. They were both like older brothers to us, sometimes correcting our childish behaviors, but always gentle and kind.

One Crack Too Many

Seeking a different adventure, Jimmy and I decided to hitch hike to Alton, Illinois, a large town about forty miles south of Palmyra. Luck was with us and it only took a couple of different rides until we were in downtown Alton, watching cars drive over the bridge that crossed into Missouri. After an hour or so, we decided to head north toward home so as not to be late. We spent what little money we had on a bag of Fritos, and stuck out our thumbs. We tried and tried to hitch a ride, but to no avail. As we were walking up the steep Alton hill, two neighborhood boys, both older than us, confronted us and demanded our bags of corn chips. We didn't want to give them up but, at Jimmy's urging, we finally obliged, and then hurriedly got out of harm's way, jogging all the way to upper Alton. We were now tired, hungry, and desperate to catch a ride, as time was not in our favor. Luckily, we spotted a familiar truck coming in our direction, and as we yelled, "Charlie," he slowed down and waited for us to catch up. Fortunately, Charlie March was heading back to Hettick and volunteered to take us all the way to Palmyra. What a friend, indeed! As we were passing Monticello College in Godfrey (a girl's school), Charlie nonchalantly mentioned that the school was closing. When we asked why, Charlie said, "Because it is full of cracks!" We didn't catch the drift, sorry to say, and didn't realize that Charlie was making a joke.

Monticello College in Godfrey-currently Lewis & Clark Community College

Later that week at supper, as I was telling Dad and Mom about our adventure, Dad remarked that I should let him know from now on before we leave town. (It was quite common for people to hitch hike during that period of time). I didn't include the incident of the two thugs demanding our treats, but I saw no harm in sharing Charlie's story about the school being 'full of cracks'. Mom gasped, Roger laughed, and Dad smacked my lips, causing them too slightly bleed. I asked to be excused, went outside and cried because I didn't know why Dad hit me. Dad came outside to speak to me and realized that I had not understood Charlie's joke.

He put his arm around my shoulders and said, "Lawrencie-boy, Charlie March thought you knew about words like that." After hearing Dad's explanation, I understood his reaction. That day was a time of learning and growing up. Later that evening Dad asked if I wanted to take a ride in his car, scouting for ground hog dens in area pond dams. Dad was strict but he also would show his love for us three boys!

Move to Terry Park

Jimmy Scantling and I spent lots of time together during the 1953-'54 school year and I was sorry to hear that his family was moving out of town. Actually, their move was only a couple of miles away, to the Terry Park Golf Course, just east of Palmyra. The Scantlings were hired as the new groundskeepers for one of the most popular golf courses in the area. Whenever I went out to visit Jimmy, I marveled at the sight of the entire family (Jimmy had a brother and three sisters) doing their daily chores. Mr. Scantling still worked at the Virden coal mine, so the rest of the family had to carry a big part of the workload.

Secret Door

I frequently visited Jimmy at Terry Park and sometimes I helped rake sand greens, earning myself a free round of golf. On one occasion, when we were alone in the old Terry house, Jimmy showed me a trap door in one of the closets. Using a flashlight, we looked down into an old deserted basement room. An old ladder was attached to the wooden floor frame so we slowly climbed down the ladder, breaking its last rung as we touched the ground. Jimmy said that Mayor Oral Cooper told his parents about the secret room being used as a haven for run-away slaves, reputedly as a part of the Underground Railroad System. There were buttons, various pottery items, and some old clothes, but we left everything in place. We also saw several fallen beams that covered a tunnel opening that was blocked by timber, rocks, and dirt. After we exited the hidden room, Jimmy told me not to say anything about our venture, as his Dad told the family that the secret room was off limits.

High School: Junior and Senior Years

My last two years at Northwestern High School were fun and successful as academics became more important to me. Everyone, both teachers and students, seemed to "get along," thanks to Mr. Lester J. Cox, our principal. He always seemed to be one step ahead of all the trouble makers, which probably created his nickname, "Sly Fox." Our family was loyal supporters of all athletics, and, of course, Mom's music performances, and we attended most school events or activities.

Watching the Wildcats

Lacking athletic talent didn't keep me from becoming an avid sports fan, and I looked forward to attending as many home/ away games as my parents would allow. We boys were aware that Dad was a stickler for being on time, so we were always ready for his command, "Let's go!" During my sophomore and junior years, the Northwestern basketball team was the talk of the town. The 1954 starting team (Harold Weller, Jack Kemp, Morris Hicks, Larry Redfern, and Marvin Turner) won fifteen games, including the district tournament at Girard. The following year Marvin Turner, Larry Redfern, Ralph March, Gary Thomas, and Bob Morehead led the 1955 Wildcats to thirteen victories. The 1954 and 1955 football teams were also excellent as they recorded 5-3 seasons.

1953 Northwestern Basketball Team
Kneeling L-R: Lawrence Weller, Delbert Garner,
Larry Redfern, Morris Hicks, Marvin Turner.
Standing L-R: Coach, Cecil McVey, Coy Grimmett,
Harold Weller, Ronald Duncan, Jim Waters,
Jack Kemp, Rex Redfern

*1954 Northwestern Basketball District Champions
L-R: Larry Redfern, Morris Hicks, Marvin Turner,
Harold Weller, Jack Kemp*

To the Rescue

The bridge at Terry Park Lake, 1954

Jimmy and I loved to fish off of the old wooden bridge that spanned a narrow part of the lake at Terry Park. On Sunday, June 13, 1954, as we were walking toward the bridge, a man shouted for our help. As we ran toward the bridge we could see a young boy floundering in the water, some eight feet from shore. We both jumped into the lake and with our combined efforts, we were able to rescue the six year old lad. We pulled him from the lake and after a few chest compressions he coughed and began to cry. The boy's father, Mr. Dan Daily of Auburn, Illinois, could not swim and was elated that we had saved his son, Don. He offered us a nice reward but we declined to accept because we were so proud that we had saved this little boy's life.

Dairy Farm Adventures

My first steady job began in the summer of 1954 when I was hired to work at Fred Rupple's dairy farm. Because I didn't have a driver's license, Dad drove me to Fred's farm, located three miles south of Palmyra. Arriving at 6:45 a.m., I began filling the milk cooler with the raw milk from the fifteen dairy cows.

Later, I was assigned the messy task of removing manure from the walk ways and the milking stations. After the morning milking was finished, we usually repaired fence or did custom hay baling for neighboring farmers. My day's work usually ended just after the evening milking and either Dad or Mom would be there at 5:00 p.m. for my ride home. My pay for the week's work was $36.00, including the biggest noon meals that I could imagine. I was rich!

Snakes Alive: We were baling hay for Clarence Ward on one summer day when snakes were on the move. Clarence had hired three workers to help load and unload hay wagons. As we all worked together on a hot summer day, we noticed that Johnny Eyer was afraid of snakes and yelled at the very sight of one. We began yelling "snake" just to see his reactions. Then the worst possible thing happened-someone tossed a dead snake over the wagon and it landed on Johnny's shoulder. He let out a blood curdling scream and started chasing me. I wasn't the guilty party (that time), but I knew better than to try reasoning with Johnny. I'm glad he was overweight and I was faster.

One Well Was Enough: The old well at the dairy farm was not dependable during the dry season, so Fred hired a 'well-witcher' to locate a good water source. We began digging a new well by hand using spades, and recent rains made the early going rather easy. After digging to a four foot depth, we installed a ladder into the hole and then carried five gallon buckets of dirt to the top. When a ten foot depth had been reached, Fred devised a homemade tripod just above the well opening. A set of pulleys with a large rope was attached to the tripod and we were in business. Using a small tractor, we hoisted a large steel bucket, filled with dirt to the top of the well opening. At that point a hook pole was used to swing the bucket away from the well, depositing eight to ten gallons of dirt to the side of the hole. Fred and I took turns digging in the well until one afternoon a chunk of dirt fell from the top ledge, hitting my arm. Upon seeing the bruise, Dad told Fred he didn't want me digging in the hole anymore. Fred agreed and I became the engineer at the top. I missed digging beneath the ground on those July days as the temperature was much cooler in the well than shoveling dirt above the hole. Fred hit a spring of water at about twenty feet and then he began making a rock and concrete foundation. Then as I lowered regular bricks on a large wooden platform, Fred 'bricked' the walls all the way to the top. The 'witcher' had indeed picked a good spot and Fred's water problems were solved.

Ruppleʼs Dairy Barn, 1954

Front Porch Delivery: After the morning milking, we would skim the previous dayʼs milk, removing cream for town customers. After the raw milk was bottled, I drove Fredʼs old car, delivering milk to the many customers in a three mile radius. On one particular day as I was delivering milk to Jack and Donna Mitch, I applied the brakes as usual, but the brake line broke. I was terrified as the car smashed through the front yard picket fence and came to rest at the edge of the porch. Mrs. Mitch came rushing out of the house visibly upset and with words to match. I couldnʼt think of what to say, so I blurted out, "Front door delivery!" Astonished by my remark, and after hearing my explanation, she finally accepted my apology. Fred arrived to repair the brake line and then we all enjoyed a cup of coffee and a good laugh. The Mitch family never let me forget those milk delivery days and my one "special" delivery.

Saved by a Clay Bowl: After years of reading about Indians and looking for artifacts, I decided to do the ultimate thing. I informed the barber, Red Luttrell, that I wanted something different, a 'Mohawk' haircut. Red said, "A what!" I explained that he would cut my hair as short as possible on all sides, leaving an inch wide strip of hair from the forehead to the neck. Red said very firmly, "Paul will not approve of that." I told Red that I was paying for the haircut and that is what I wanted. "OK," said Red, "but don't blame me!" Later that day, after Dad had walked home from his store, Roger 'spilled the beans' as we played outside. After supper I started to go back outside and resume play, but Dad told me to get in the car, that we were going for a ride. Unbeknownst to me, he had called Red, and soon there I was, settling in the barber's chair again. Red stated, "I told you, Larry!" Dad told Red to cut off the 'Mohawk' strip of hair and then shave my entire head. I thought that was pretty neat until the next day when Dad drove me to work at Rupple's Dairy Farm. As I reached for my hat and gloves, Dad grabbed my hat, saying, "You won't need this today, Lawrencie boy!" I replied, "Yes, I will, because we will be baling hay." Dad was adamant. "You should have thought about that before you made an a-- of yourself." As I walked into the milking barn, Fred greeted me with these words, "Larry, don't ask to use any of my hats today. Your Dad called last night about your haircut." 'Twas one of Dad's teaching moments!

Later, as we were baling hay at Hobert Vogel's farm, the sun began to burn the top of my head. During mid-morning break I thought of a possible remedy and trotted off to a nearby creek, where I found a strain of gray clay in the bank. I mixed the clay with hay stubble, fashioning it into a bowl until the top of my head was entirely covered. Throughout the day I would remove and reinforce the bowl, wetting it down to preserve its resilience. This perseverance saved the day.

When Dad arrived at 5:00 p.m., Fred beat me to his car, saying, "Paul, I didn't give Larry a hat to wear." He went on to tell the entire story and as I entered the car I expected the worst. After driving about two miles in silence, Dad broke down laughing, saying, "Damn you, Lawrencie-boy, that's the cleverest thing I ever heard." Dad let me off the hook and I felt so good to have received his forgiveness.

Jiggling Headlights

Saturday night curfew was generally set at 11:00 p.m., but when Mom and Dad visited friends after the store closed, I frequently extended my free time. One Saturday night (November 20, 1954) I was invited to go to Carlinville with Wayne Crum and Warren Williams to check out the action on the square. With a guarantee of being home by midnight, we headed south on State Road 111. As we passed the junction with State Road 108 that headed west toward Greenfield, I noticed an oncoming car's headlights jiggle, followed by darkness. I told my friends what I had seen, but they weren't concerned. As we approached the Carlinville 'Y', I again mentioned the possibility of a wreck and the fact that someone might need our help. Finally, at my insistence, we turned around and drove to the area where I last saw the car's headlights. Upon reaching the scene we instantly realized that there had, indeed, been an accident. I quickly exited our car and was the first to view the horrible wreck. The car had crashed, hitting a guard rail, driving the vertical plank beside the steering column through the young man's stomach. The impact broke out the front seat and the impaled driver ended up sitting upright in the back seat. We were devastated by what we saw and knew that this was a mortal injury. We quickly drove to a farm house, where a call was made to the Macoupin County police. Later, an ambulance arrived to carry the body of Lyndel E. VanBebber of Scottville to the Carlinville Hospital, where he was officially declared dead. As the ambulance left, we headed back home instead of continuing to Carlinville. Our hearts were heavy that Saturday night.

Dad's Hot Chevy

Dad's "Hot" Chevy, 1955

Dad bought a new BelAire Chevrolet, (2-door, hardtop) in 1955. It was the classiest car around. The V-8, 283 HP with a power pack, also quickly became known as the 'hottest' car around---until Dad found out, that is!

The Diane Drive-In movie theater opened in 1952 and quickly became popular for young folks and families alike. One evening as cars were leaving the outdoor theater, Charlie Crum and Dale Leach were planning a race from the nearby Richman curve, heading west to the Carlinville 'Y', located at the junction of S.R. 111. Dale's car, a Mercury, and Charlie's car, a Ford, were both touted as two of the faster cars in the area. That's where Dad's car came in! I closely followed Dale and Charlie as they began their quest for victory, waiting for my chance to show off Dad's car. The final two miles of State Road 108 were straight and clear, so I decided to make my move. Within a half mile of junction State Road 111, I passed both cars and the victory was mine. Or so I thought! The next day after store hours, Dad questioned me about Friday night's adventure. Charlie Crum had told him that his hardtop Chevy took top honors and he wanted an explanation. Knowing better than to lie, I confessed, also knowing that borrowing Dad's car from then on would come with stringent rules and regulations. Durn you, Charlie!

All Clear

When attending the Diane Drive-In, we sometimes let one person hide in the trunk. Upon entering the Drive-In, just prior to the start of the movie, we would drive to the back row, letting the "freebie" know when it was safe to exit the trunk and enter the car. On one occasion it was Jimmy Scantling's turn for a "freebie". Instead of going to the back row, I drove to the front most parking spot, giving Jimmy the "all clear" signal. As Jimmy exited the trunk in full view of everyone, the other patrons began blowing their horns and flashing their lights. Jimmy jumped in the car, laughing with everyone else, stating, "You guys set me up." Even though the joke was on Jimmy, he took it in stride. We rewarded him later with a free burger and fries at England's Drive-In in Hettick, and kept our friendship as strong as ever.

Boondockin'

Abandoned railroad right-a-ways and remote township roads provided excellent locations for moonlight romance. It became the talk of the town when a couple was caught "parking" late at night. That's where the four musketeers came in! Our practice was to meet at Hargett's Drug Store after taking our dates home for the evening. We soon discovered the popular parking spots and the game was on. Gary March was the first to use the word, 'boondockin,' and it caught on as a popular term around school. On one occasion, as we were leaving England's Drive-In, we observed taillights on the old railroad bed just north of Richie Road. We drove past, and then backtracked with our lights turned off. We parked at the entrance to Richie Road, climbed out the open windows, and crept about one hundred yards to the parked car. On command we jumped up on the front bumper and then took off toward our own car. The driver of the parked car immediately turned on his headlights and came roaring down the old road bed, catching us before we could reach our car. Blackberry bushes lined both sides of the road, but with the 1954 Chevy car barreling towards us, and no time to spare, we jumped into the tangled berries. With many cuts as evidence, we took a lot of teasing the next week at school.

When Dale Schramm started to miss our weekly

boondockin' assignments, we began to suspect one of our very own. The remaining musketeers made plans to verify our suspicions, mapping routes and drawing diagrams of possible locations. Each one of us secured our individual territory at the appropriate time and the challenge was on! After several weeks of coming up short, we had to change our strategy. Instead of driving the back roads in desperation, we decided to hide in various locations and wait for the 1950 Chevy to come to us. Still no success! Then, after a few more weeks, a break in the action finally came through. The blue and white Chevy was seen heading north from Palmyra, but it never arrived in Modesto, or on the back road leading to Terry Park. One afternoon, after an intensive examination of that general area, I spotted an old abandoned farm house about half way between Palmyra and Modesto, located on the east side of State Road 111. A seldom used lane road led to the house and garage. Bingo! When the next opportunity arrived, we were ready. As we approached the deserted farmstead, we turned off our lights and quietly drove two hundred yards down the lane road. The old, rickety garage had two wooden hinged doors that were closed, and parked inside was the 1950 Chevy. We yelled and beat on the garage walls, then quickly exited the scene. Mystery solved and a job well done! Later, we all had a big laugh and our friendship remained as strong as ever.

Who's Going Home Now?

Saturday nights in Standard City were not for the "faint hearted!" Standard City a very small village (less than five hundred people in the 1950s) with big city envisions that included four active taverns and 'other' possible entertainment. We never stopped along the strip establishments as we drove through town, except for one occasion. Noticing a large crowd outside one tavern, we could see a fight taking place that included Kenny Stults, a good friend of mine. We made our way to the outside perimeter and watched as Kenny was taking a beating from a giant of a person. The obvious winner walked off, boasting to Kenny that he had better go home. As soon as he heard those words, Kenny arose from the ground and ran after the larger man, jumping on his back and throwing him to the ground. Kenny grabbed the guy's head and began smashing it in the rock parking lot. Things got so bloody that bystanders had to pull Kenny off the helpless opponent. As Kenny stood victorious, he slapped his hands together, and with a firm and taunting voice, recounted the perfect words, "Now, who should be going home!" We boys were thrilled by the outcome, and I was especially proud because Kenny was one of my heroes. Kenny always went out of his way to greet me when I was young and I felt extra special when he called me "little Shorty," after my dad.

The Big 100

Palmyra celebrated its 100th year anniversary on July 23 - 24, 1955, in a big way. Mayor Oral Cooper, the village board, and several local committees worked hard for several months preparing for the celebration. Visitors came from far and wide as the parade featured antique cars, floats, horses, Indians, area school bands, and dances. There were also competition races, skill related challenges, and a variety of food.

Jimmy Scantling and me riding horses in the Palmyra Centennial Parade, 1955

Trucks in Palmyra Centennial Parade

Martha (Ross) March in Palmyra Centennial Parade

*Parade dignitaries, Mayor Clyde Stevenson
and Oral Cooper*

*Drum Major and Honor Guard in
Palmyra Centennial Parade*

Men who grew beards for the Centennial Celebration

Headless Driver

We were always trying to think of ways to impress the older guys that 'hung-out' at Hargett's Drug Store. Jimmy Scantling and I came up with a winner of an idea as we waited for the perfect opportunity, on a warm summer night. Several young men were loafing outside Hargett's store and there were very few vehicles to be seen. Jimmy and I left from the north edge of town, with Jimmy lying down in the front seat, operating the gas and brake pedal with one hand and steering with the other. I was seated on the right side, waving out the window and yelling to the guys. At the same time, I was instructing Jimmy as to turning and slowing down. As we made the next approach, the Hargett gang moved closer to the road to get a better look, saying things like, "Where's the driver?" Twice was enough as we spotted Adam Fetter, night watchman, making his rounds. Our one night stand brought us attention and laughter, but we wisely gave up any further performances of our dangerous prank.

The Haunted Barn

Halloween was a fun time for most families and also a time for scary tricks. One of our gang thought of an ingenious Halloween prank of making a ghost, consisting of a sheet covering a balloon with face markings, to scare "parkers." An old abandoned barn near Irving Tongate's farm was chosen as the site for our ingenious prank. We took a few measurements, nailed a wire from the hay loft opening to a tree located near the barn, and attached our ghost to the wire with a steel hook. The boyfriend half of the selected couples was informed of the stunt and everything was scheduled to accommodate multiple visitors. We eagerly awaited the guests as they drove up the lane road and parked near the front of the old barn. After a few minutes someone would push the attached ghost out the loft door, giving a blood curdling yell as the ghost slid down the wire. A shrill cry from the girlfriend in the parked car was all it took to make our night and we were rewarded on several occasions.

Arkansas Bound

Jimmy Scantling was one of my closest friends since he moved to Palmyra in 1953. Together we shared many happy times full of laughter, with a few pranks and thrills thrown in for excitement. To our credit, though, we were among the first to volunteer when someone needed our help. Even so, there seemed to be something missing in our lives, a void that we both knew was there but seldom talked about.

Jimmy's father, Jim, was a great provider for his family, but working full time at the coal mine and trying to manage the Terry Park golf course took its toll. Jim's drinking was becoming a problem, so Dorothy, his wife, worked extra hard keeping the family busy taking care of the golf course. She also made sure that the family attended the Palmyra Baptist Church on a regular basis, helping to keep the family strong.

The Mahan home was admired as an ideal family, but in truth it wasn't. Mom and Dad loved we three boys and we were raised to be kind and respectable. We were afforded many opportunities and activities that provided for a happy home, but Mom and Dad seldom showed love for each other. Dad had his store business and his hunting to keep him satisfied while Mother enjoyed teaching music and chauffeuring her lady friends to musicals and on shopping outings. Dad didn't need lots of people around, while Mother enjoyed a multitude of social events. Mother's childhood trauma continued to haunt her for many of her adult years, which helped to explain her insecurity. I often dreamed of leaving home and being on my own, but I had no idea what the future had in store.

Larry, 1955

Jimmy Scantling, 1955

Jimmy and I were both soul searching as we tried to "grow up," but sometimes our adventures and decisions took us on the wrong pathway. In October of 1955, Jimmy decided to make the daring decision to leave home at the start of his junior year. Without notifying anyone, Jimmy, lacking a driver's license, but possessing an old car that he had purchased for $35.00, took off for his aunt's home in Booneville, Arkansas. Jimmy enrolled in the Booneville Schools, hoping to fill that void in his life. I was shocked by Jimmy's departure, but I understood his feelings of low self-esteem, something that I also felt. I sure missed him as I continued my senior year at Northwestern, one filled with uncertainties.

Feathers of the Red Rooster

The King and Queen carnival was an annual event that helped raise money for the senior class trip. Tickets were sold for such activities as dart and hoop throws, basketball shots, and other skill games. Also a variety of foods, donated by community supporters, provided a popular menu for the many patrons.

The class of 1956 spent several evenings building props for the big event, leaving the night before the carnival free to spend preparing food for the luscious meal. Mrs. Eblen, bookkeeping teacher, had graciously donated a live chicken to be used for chicken salad sandwiches. We forgot about Mrs. Eblen's contribution until late evening, so Norman Gibbs and I hurriedly drove to her residence. Seeing that the lights were out, we assumed that Mrs. Eblen had gone to bed. Not wanting to disturb her, I suggested that we go ahead and obtain a chicken from the back yard coop. I grabbed the first chicken that I saw and that turned out to be the wrong decision! That night after all preparations had been completed, the planning committee left for their homes on a positive note.

The day of the carnival was met with anticipation as we prepared for the big night. Then, just after the first period class had started, Mr. Cox called a meeting with our planning committee. The first thing he said was, "Who went to Mrs. Eblen's house to get the chicken?" Norman and I immediately raised our hands, not thinking that we had done anything wrong. It was then that we found out that the chicken I took was, unfortunately, Mrs. Eblen's pet rooster. We explained what happened and Mr. Cox seemed to understand, as he shook his head in despair. He told us that Mrs. Eblen had stayed home from school, heartbroken and upset that her red rooster had been taken. I was instructed to walk over to Mrs. Eblen's residence, explain what happened, and ask for her forgiveness. I thoughtfully prepared my story as I walked those two long blocks, ready to receive a scolding. To my surprise, Mrs. Eblen understood as she accepted my sincere apology. After a big hug and a few shed tears, Mrs. Eblen appeared to feel much better and I left to return to school. Later, Mrs. Eblen even made a joke about the incident, willing "the feathers of the red rooster to Larry Mahan." That's when I truly felt forgiven.

A Plate for Two and Heartaches by the Number

England's Drive-In, Hettick, Illinois

England's Drive-In in Hettick was a favorite eating place for people of all ages. Visitors came from several miles to sample their huge burgers, a plate full of french fries, and hand-dipped milkshakes served in a large metal canister. It was a common sight to see young couples make an order and then split the full meal deal, all for a dollar. An added attraction was the jukebox that housed all the favorite songs of the day. Young girls would literally pack around the jukebox on Saturday nights as they selected three songs for a quarter. Some of the songs on the hit list included, Bye, Bye Love (Everly Brothers); My Special Angel (Bobby Helms); Young Love (Sonny James); Don't Be Cruel (Elvis Presley); There Stands the Glass (Webb Pierce); Your Cheatin' Heart (Hank Williams); Four Walls (Jim Reeves); I Walk the Line (Johnny Cash); Heartaches by the Number (Ray Price); Tennessee Waltz (Patti Page); A White Sport Coast and a Pink Carnation (Marty Robbins). Those were just a few love songs that remained popular for many years. Occasionally a young girl would break out into tears after hearing a song that reminded her of a relationship that had ended.

And the Winner is…

The Illinois Theater in Jacksonville, Illinois was a popular place to see other friends on a date. One time, after meeting Dale Schramm and his date, my date and I prepared to leave for home. Dale asked which route I was taking to Palmyra and I responded that I was taking State Road 104 to State Road 111, then south to Modesto. Dale boasted that driving south on State Road 67 to the Scottville blacktop and across to Modesto was shorter in time. So we bet a milkshake as to who would arrive first. After we agreed to drive at a maximum speed of sixty mph, we left from the corner of Morton and State Streets at the same time. The game was on! Knowing that Dale would exceed the agreed upon speed limit, I turned around after a block and began chasing his car. After approximately ten miles I could see, in the distance, the tiny brake lights that were distinctive to Dale's 1950 Chevy. I slowed down to avoid suspicion. As Dale turned on the Scottville Road, I paused, and then also headed down the Scottville Road, but with my headlights turned off. By the light of the moon, we followed within a couple hundred yards, using the hand brake when necessary to slow down. Driving seventy to seventy five mph is a challenge but as luck would have it, I didn't meet any other cars on the Scottville/ Modesto Road. I caught up with Dale just as we approached the Modesto square, turning on my headlights and tooting the horn. Later, as we sat in Hargett's Drug Store drinking our milkshakes, Dale couldn't get over my sneaky trick. Drinking that free milkshake made it even better!

Adam to the Rescue

Several of "the gang" decided it would be cool to share a jug of Morgan David wine. We were not of age so a friend made the purchase for us at a tavern in Hettick. We realized that what we were doing was illegal but we drove to Oak Hill Cemetery and consumed the entire bottle. Later, as I started toward home, I began to feel sick. Knowing that my curfew time was rapidly approaching, I contacted Adam Fetter, the night watchman for Palmyra. Adam could tell that I was "not feeling well" as he volunteered to help me out "this once." Adam and Dad were very good friends and frequently Adam would park in our drive way, toot his horn, and wait for Dad to come out and visit. I waited for Adam to make his move, and then I parked the Chevy in the garage and made a quick exit towards the house. I felt a little better until I went to bed, then everything started going 'round and round.' I stood up which made things better, but as I lay down again, everything reverted back to spinning. I had to make a quick dash to the upstairs porch window, depositing the contents of my stomach on the roof. I finally got to sleep and the next day I carried buckets of water to clean off the shingles as best I could. Later as I was thanking Adam for his help, he shared stories of other incidences such as that which didn't end on a positive note. I thanked Adam and gave him a big hug before I left his home.

Post Script: Ten years later when I was visiting my parents, Dad asked me if I would like to help spot ground hogs that were invading Willis DeWitt's pond dam. Eager to please Dad, we drove to within one hundred yards of the pond dam and waited for ground hogs to emerge. Dad made two successful kills, and then gave the 243 rifle to me. Just as I was taking aim with the scope, Dad blurted out, "Can you see any better now, than you did the night that you came home sick on Morgan David wine?" Aghast, I couldn't believe that Dad knew about that incident all these years and didn't say anything about it. Dad explained that Adam made him promise to let me 'off the hook' that time because he felt that I had learned a valuable lesson. Adam was right, as I never put myself in such a predicament again. Thanks, Adam!

Nassa Creek Calls

When time permitted I continued to visit the Nassa Creek area looking for Indian Artifacts. Whenever Dad's old hunting car was available I drove a different route, parking at the old Maud Hoff farmstead. From the old abandoned farm home, I could see our old farm place to the west and the McGuire farm to the south. I usually started walking one direction and then returned the other way. The best times to hunt were after fall plowing and during the early spring rainy season and I continued to find choice artifacts.

Indian Stone Tools

I often carried my trusted 410 shotgun, always looking for wild game to help fill Dutch Brown's freezer. Dutch's health was slowly deteriorating but, as usual, he was so appreciative of my visits.

The Dandelion Saga

We knew better than to skip school, but during the spring of 1956, Dale Schramm and I conceived a perfect plan for a free day from high school. I told Mom and Dad that the Schramm's had invited me to spend the upcoming Thursday night with Dale and they gave their permission. As we (supposedly) left for school on that Friday morning, we headed for Springfield, Illinois instead in Dale's 1950 Chevy. We eventually arrived in downtown Springfield and walked around the square viewing the sights. Just before noon as we were approaching Fishman's Sporting Goods, Dale let out a sudden moan as he caught sight of Mr. Cox, our principal, walking toward us. Cringing, we quickly turned our backs and began looking into a business showcase window, hoping not to be seen. As Mr. Cox passed by he calmly said, "Good morning, boys." Dale wasn't sure that he knew who we were but I thought otherwise. We quickly left the scene and headed home. (Later we learned that Mr. Cox went to Springfield each year about that time to purchase sports awards for the athletic banquet).

Dad and Mr. Cox were good friends, so I was quite sure that Dad would hear about the adventure before the day was out. To my surprise, nothing was said that weekend, but I knew things would come to a head on Monday. Both our girlfriends had written excuse notes, so we delivered the fake notes first thing Monday morning to Henrietta Hoover, the office secretary. I "smelled a rat" when she quickly excused our absences, without any questions or comments. We expected a 'call to the office' during Monday, but nothing happened. Then, after Tuesday, Wednesday, and Thursday came and went without any office intervention, Dale repeated his thought that there was a chance that Mr. Cox had not recognized us after all. Friday was a stressful day, as each period passed ever so slowly. During 8th period, I watched the clock on the wall, eagerly awaiting the 3:30 dismissal bell. Then, at 3:25, Mr. Cox walked into the study hall and as he passed my table, he quietly spoke, asking me to stop by the office after school. The suspense was finally over!

Mr. Cox greeted Dale and me after school with a pleasant reaction, "OK guys, you know why you are here, so let's resolve this problem together!" Cox began by saying that he appreciated our attitude at school, our above average grades, and the fact that we had not caused any problems in the past year. He went on to say that our parents had been informed (gulp!) that we had "volunteered" to work on the school buildings and grounds project immediately after school. We had no idea what the "project" entailed, but we both felt a little sigh of relief. Mr. Cox carried a large wooden box as we followed him to the school yard, adjacent to the south side of the building. His instructions were quite simple—pick dandelion heads (no stems what-so-ever) and fill the box and when the box was full, "You may go home." We quickly began the tedious job and within a half hour the box was almost full. Mr. Cox appeared on the scene, praised our efforts, then stepped into the box, crushing the dandelion heads and severely lessening our efforts. After several repeated visits and two hours of boring and backbreaking work, our "volunteer" service was completed. Mr. Cox chuckled as he praised our efforts, as only Mr. Cox could do. During the evening supper meal, Dad praised my volunteering at school and stated that he was very proud of me. Could it be that he really didn't know the truth?

Post Script: Two years later, while attending Macomb State Teacher's College, I came home for the weekend. At a family meal I casually mentioned the fact that several of my college friends often skipped classes. Dad, with a smile on his face, quickly responded by saying, "Maybe they will have to pick dandelion heads after school!" He had known all along and waited for the right time to share his well-kept secret. There was no outsmarting Dad or "the sly fox!"

Working for the Government

Government Grain Bins, 1956

Working at Rupple's Dairy had been a great experience and I appreciated a chance for a steady job. Then, in the spring of 1956, I applied for a job with the United States Department of Agriculture (USDA). The work entailed repairing government grain bins located throughout Macoupin County, Illinois, and the pay was an eye popping $2.85 per hour. A few weeks later I got a call from Clarence Whittler of Girard, informing me that I had been selected as one of three young men from the Palmyra area to work during the summer months. Later, I found out that Dad and Mr. Whittler had been close friends for several years. Good old politics!

My normal day at work involved riding around with Mr. Whittler to various bin sites as we inspected them for grain delivery. Sometimes we checked bins that contained corn to make sure that a crust had not formed on the top of the corn. If a crust had developed, the air flow would be limited, thus causing a heat build-up that could create mold. I became the official "stirrer" as I slipped into my safety harness and began stirring the top foot layer of corn. A rope was attached to my harness and Mr. Whittler gave me just enough slack to finish the entire job. I frequently suggested to Mr. Whittler that I didn't see the need for the harness, until one day I stepped on the crust of a small vacuum hole. I immediately sank to my waist and with every movement I settled a little deeper. Clarence was a rather large and stout person and he had no trouble pulling me to safety. As we rested on a concrete ledge, I thanked Mr. Whittler, and I never complained about safety issues again.

A Fork in the Road

During my senior year in high school I was filled with doubt and uncertainty. My buddy, Jimmy Scantling, had moved to Arkansas, my other close friends were making plans for their own futures, and I was ready for a major change in my life. My parents could detect a sense of urgency on my part and that's when Dad and Mom stepped forth and stated emphatically that I was going to college. Two of my classmates had already enrolled at Macomb State Teacher's College so I decided to visit that campus. Within a few weeks after being accepted by the college, I officially registered in the field of general education for the coming year. I had no idea what was in store for me, but I welcomed the challenge.

Larry's Senior Graduation Picture

Postscript:

During my college years, and then later in my adult life, I frequently reminisced about my childhood memories. Some were unpleasant, but most involved the three 'L's'- learning, laughter, and love. I have a lot to be thankful for, especially those special people who helped me mature during my childhood. As an expression of gratitude, I give thanks to the following people who taught me about the lessons of life:

1. *Mom & Dad*- Be on time, no hurtful teasing, honor the young and the old, look to help others, and love your work (as Mom, especially, did).
2. *Harold Maguire*- Patience. After I hurriedly walked over a few arrowheads, Harold helped me to slow down, be more observant, and enjoy the moment.
3. *Dutch Brown*- Appreciate nature. Dutch helped to create an interest in nature, and the serenity that it provides.
4. *Fred Rupple*- Resilience. Even during hard times, Fred remained a happy and positive person.
5. *Marvin Pence, Bill Holloway, Harold Richie, Kenny Stults, and Bob Nifong*- Encouragement for young kids. Thanks for making me feel important by your acts of kindness.
6. *Adam Fetter*- Responsibility. Even though you could be rough and gruff your teachings were appreciated.
7. *Jimmy Scantling*- An excellent role model, someone who didn't gossip, got along with everyone, and became my best friend.
8. *Lester J. Cox*- As a teacher and principal you were the best. Your disciplinary tactics never gave more punishment than was warranted, and no one ever got the better of "the sly fox!"

About the Author

Lawrence (Larry) Powell Mahan was born in Palmyra, Illinois on December 19, 1938. He attended grade school at Palmyra (grades 1-6), and Hettick (grades 7-8), and graduated from Northwestern High School (Palmyra) in 1956.

Larry received his Bachelor of Science degree in 1960 from Western Illinois University (Macomb), and a Masters in Administration degree from the University of Illinois (Springfield) in 1978.

Larry taught for fifty years in several schools including, Rockridge (Reynolds, Illinois); San Bernardino, California; Palmyra, Illinois (teacher and principal); New Berlin, Illinois (principal), and Christian Elementary School (Springfield, Illinois).

In 2002, Larry authored a book entitled, *In Search of Large Trees*, and in 2013, he and his wife, Donna, co-authored a travel guide book, *20 Day Trips in and around the Shawnee National Forest*, that was named Best Travel Guide of 2013, by *Booklist* magazine.

Larry and Donna now reside just south of Palmyra, Illinois on a twenty acre farm, where they have planted over one hundred and fifty trees at their Mahan Arboretum.